## Contact details

_____

_____

_____

# SCORE SHEET

| EVENT | | DATE | |
|---|---|---|---|
| ROUND | | BOARD | |
| SECTION | | OPENING | |
| **WHITE (name of player)** | | **BLACK (name of player)** | |

| | White | Black | | White | Black | | White | Black |
|---|---|---|---|---|---|---|---|---|
| 1 | | | 21 | | | 41 | | |
| 2 | | | 22 | | | 42 | | |
| 3 | | | 23 | | | 43 | | |
| 4 | | | 24 | | | 44 | | |
| 5 | | | 25 | | | 45 | | |
| 6 | | | 26 | | | 46 | | |
| 7 | | | 27 | | | 47 | | |
| 8 | | | 28 | | | 48 | | |
| 9 | | | 29 | | | 49 | | |
| 10 | | | 30 | | | 50 | | |
| 11 | | | 31 | | | 51 | | |
| 12 | | | 32 | | | 52 | | |
| 13 | | | 33 | | | 53 | | |
| 14 | | | 34 | | | 54 | | |
| 15 | | | 35 | | | 55 | | |
| 16 | | | 36 | | | 56 | | |
| 17 | | | 37 | | | 57 | | |
| 18 | | | 38 | | | 58 | | |
| 19 | | | 39 | | | 59 | | |
| 20 | | | 40 | | | 60 | | |

## RESULTS

___ WHITE WON          ___ DRAW          ___ BLACK WON

Notes

SIGNATURE                    SIGNATURE

# SCORE SHEET

| EVENT | | DATE | |
|---|---|---|---|
| ROUND | | BOARD | |
| SECTION | | OPENING | |
| **WHITE (name of player)** | | **BLACK (name of player)** | |

| | White | Black | | White | Black | | White | Black |
|---|---|---|---|---|---|---|---|---|
| 1 | | | 21 | | | 41 | | |
| 2 | | | 22 | | | 42 | | |
| 3 | | | 23 | | | 43 | | |
| 4 | | | 24 | | | 44 | | |
| 5 | | | 25 | | | 45 | | |
| 6 | | | 26 | | | 46 | | |
| 7 | | | 27 | | | 47 | | |
| 8 | | | 28 | | | 48 | | |
| 9 | | | 29 | | | 49 | | |
| 10 | | | 30 | | | 50 | | |
| 11 | | | 31 | | | 51 | | |
| 12 | | | 32 | | | 52 | | |
| 13 | | | 33 | | | 53 | | |
| 14 | | | 34 | | | 54 | | |
| 15 | | | 35 | | | 55 | | |
| 16 | | | 36 | | | 56 | | |
| 17 | | | 37 | | | 57 | | |
| 18 | | | 38 | | | 58 | | |
| 19 | | | 39 | | | 59 | | |
| 20 | | | 40 | | | 60 | | |

## RESULTS

___ WHITE WON        ___ DRAW        ___ BLACK WON

| | Notes |
|---|---|
| 8 7 6 5 4 3 2 1 A B C D E F G H | |

| SIGNATURE | | SIGNATURE | |

# SCORE SHEET

| EVENT | | DATE | |
|---|---|---|---|
| ROUND | | BOARD | |
| SECTION | | OPENING | |
| **WHITE (name of player)** | | **BLACK (name of player)** | |

| | White | Black | | White | Black | | White | Black |
|---|---|---|---|---|---|---|---|---|
| 1 | | | 21 | | | 41 | | |
| 2 | | | 22 | | | 42 | | |
| 3 | | | 23 | | | 43 | | |
| 4 | | | 24 | | | 44 | | |
| 5 | | | 25 | | | 45 | | |
| 6 | | | 26 | | | 46 | | |
| 7 | | | 27 | | | 47 | | |
| 8 | | | 28 | | | 48 | | |
| 9 | | | 29 | | | 49 | | |
| 10 | | | 30 | | | 50 | | |
| 11 | | | 31 | | | 51 | | |
| 12 | | | 32 | | | 52 | | |
| 13 | | | 33 | | | 53 | | |
| 14 | | | 34 | | | 54 | | |
| 15 | | | 35 | | | 55 | | |
| 16 | | | 36 | | | 56 | | |
| 17 | | | 37 | | | 57 | | |
| 18 | | | 38 | | | 58 | | |
| 19 | | | 39 | | | 59 | | |
| 20 | | | 40 | | | 60 | | |

## RESULTS

___ WHITE WON          ___ DRAW          ___ BLACK WON

| | Notes |
|---|---|
| 8 7 6 5 4 3 2 1<br>A B C D E F G H | |

| SIGNATURE | | SIGNATURE | |
|---|---|---|---|

# SCORE SHEET

| EVENT | | DATE | |
| ROUND | | BOARD | |
| SECTION | | OPENING | |
| **WHITE (name of player)** | | **BLACK (name of player)** | |

| | White | Black | | White | Black | | White | Black |
|---|---|---|---|---|---|---|---|---|
| 1 | | | 21 | | | 41 | | |
| 2 | | | 22 | | | 42 | | |
| 3 | | | 23 | | | 43 | | |
| 4 | | | 24 | | | 44 | | |
| 5 | | | 25 | | | 45 | | |
| 6 | | | 26 | | | 46 | | |
| 7 | | | 27 | | | 47 | | |
| 8 | | | 28 | | | 48 | | |
| 9 | | | 29 | | | 49 | | |
| 10 | | | 30 | | | 50 | | |
| 11 | | | 31 | | | 51 | | |
| 12 | | | 32 | | | 52 | | |
| 13 | | | 33 | | | 53 | | |
| 14 | | | 34 | | | 54 | | |
| 15 | | | 35 | | | 55 | | |
| 16 | | | 36 | | | 56 | | |
| 17 | | | 37 | | | 57 | | |
| 18 | | | 38 | | | 58 | | |
| 19 | | | 39 | | | 59 | | |
| 20 | | | 40 | | | 60 | | |

## RESULTS

___ WHITE WON          ___ DRAW          ___ BLACK WON

8
7
6
5
4
3
2
1
A B C D E F G H

Notes

| SIGNATURE | | SIGNATURE | |

# SCORE SHEET

| EVENT | | DATE | |
|---|---|---|---|
| ROUND | | BOARD | |
| SECTION | | OPENING | |
| **WHITE (name of player)** | | **BLACK (name of player)** | |

| | White | Black | | White | Black | | White | Black |
|---|---|---|---|---|---|---|---|---|
| 1 | | | 21 | | | 41 | | |
| 2 | | | 22 | | | 42 | | |
| 3 | | | 23 | | | 43 | | |
| 4 | | | 24 | | | 44 | | |
| 5 | | | 25 | | | 45 | | |
| 6 | | | 26 | | | 46 | | |
| 7 | | | 27 | | | 47 | | |
| 8 | | | 28 | | | 48 | | |
| 9 | | | 29 | | | 49 | | |
| 10 | | | 30 | | | 50 | | |
| 11 | | | 31 | | | 51 | | |
| 12 | | | 32 | | | 52 | | |
| 13 | | | 33 | | | 53 | | |
| 14 | | | 34 | | | 54 | | |
| 15 | | | 35 | | | 55 | | |
| 16 | | | 36 | | | 56 | | |
| 17 | | | 37 | | | 57 | | |
| 18 | | | 38 | | | 58 | | |
| 19 | | | 39 | | | 59 | | |
| 20 | | | 40 | | | 60 | | |

## RESULTS

___ WHITE WON        ___ DRAW        ___ BLACK WON

Notes

SIGNATURE                SIGNATURE

# SCORE SHEET

| EVENT | | DATE | |
|---|---|---|---|
| ROUND | | BOARD | |
| SECTION | | OPENING | |
| **WHITE (name of player)** | | **BLACK (name of player)** | |

| | White | Black | | White | Black | | White | Black |
|---|---|---|---|---|---|---|---|---|
| 1 | | | 21 | | | 41 | | |
| 2 | | | 22 | | | 42 | | |
| 3 | | | 23 | | | 43 | | |
| 4 | | | 24 | | | 44 | | |
| 5 | | | 25 | | | 45 | | |
| 6 | | | 26 | | | 46 | | |
| 7 | | | 27 | | | 47 | | |
| 8 | | | 28 | | | 48 | | |
| 9 | | | 29 | | | 49 | | |
| 10 | | | 30 | | | 50 | | |
| 11 | | | 31 | | | 51 | | |
| 12 | | | 32 | | | 52 | | |
| 13 | | | 33 | | | 53 | | |
| 14 | | | 34 | | | 54 | | |
| 15 | | | 35 | | | 55 | | |
| 16 | | | 36 | | | 56 | | |
| 17 | | | 37 | | | 57 | | |
| 18 | | | 38 | | | 58 | | |
| 19 | | | 39 | | | 59 | | |
| 20 | | | 40 | | | 60 | | |

## RESULTS

___ WHITE WON ___ DRAW ___ BLACK WON

Notes

SIGNATURE SIGNATURE

# SCORE SHEET

| EVENT | DATE |
|---|---|
| ROUND | BOARD |
| SECTION | OPENING |
| **WHITE (name of player)** | **BLACK (name of player)** |

| | White | Black | | White | Black | | White | Black |
|---|---|---|---|---|---|---|---|---|
| 1 | | | 21 | | | 41 | | |
| 2 | | | 22 | | | 42 | | |
| 3 | | | 23 | | | 43 | | |
| 4 | | | 24 | | | 44 | | |
| 5 | | | 25 | | | 45 | | |
| 6 | | | 26 | | | 46 | | |
| 7 | | | 27 | | | 47 | | |
| 8 | | | 28 | | | 48 | | |
| 9 | | | 29 | | | 49 | | |
| 10 | | | 30 | | | 50 | | |
| 11 | | | 31 | | | 51 | | |
| 12 | | | 32 | | | 52 | | |
| 13 | | | 33 | | | 53 | | |
| 14 | | | 34 | | | 54 | | |
| 15 | | | 35 | | | 55 | | |
| 16 | | | 36 | | | 56 | | |
| 17 | | | 37 | | | 57 | | |
| 18 | | | 38 | | | 58 | | |
| 19 | | | 39 | | | 59 | | |
| 20 | | | 40 | | | 60 | | |

## RESULTS

___ WHITE WON          ___ DRAW          ___ BLACK WON

Notes

| SIGNATURE | SIGNATURE |
|---|---|

# SCORE SHEET

| EVENT | DATE |
|---|---|
| ROUND | BOARD |
| SECTION | OPENING |
| **WHITE (name of player)** | **BLACK (name of player)** |

| | White | Black | | White | Black | | White | Black |
|---|---|---|---|---|---|---|---|---|
| 1 | | | 21 | | | 41 | | |
| 2 | | | 22 | | | 42 | | |
| 3 | | | 23 | | | 43 | | |
| 4 | | | 24 | | | 44 | | |
| 5 | | | 25 | | | 45 | | |
| 6 | | | 26 | | | 46 | | |
| 7 | | | 27 | | | 47 | | |
| 8 | | | 28 | | | 48 | | |
| 9 | | | 29 | | | 49 | | |
| 10 | | | 30 | | | 50 | | |
| 11 | | | 31 | | | 51 | | |
| 12 | | | 32 | | | 52 | | |
| 13 | | | 33 | | | 53 | | |
| 14 | | | 34 | | | 54 | | |
| 15 | | | 35 | | | 55 | | |
| 16 | | | 36 | | | 56 | | |
| 17 | | | 37 | | | 57 | | |
| 18 | | | 38 | | | 58 | | |
| 19 | | | 39 | | | 59 | | |
| 20 | | | 40 | | | 60 | | |

## RESULTS

___ WHITE WON        ___ DRAW        ___ BLACK WON

Notes

```
8
7
6
5
4
3
2
1
  A B C D E F G H
```

| SIGNATURE | SIGNATURE |
|---|---|

# SCORE SHEET

| EVENT | | DATE | |
|---|---|---|---|
| ROUND | | BOARD | |
| SECTION | | OPENING | |
| **WHITE (name of player)** | | **BLACK (name of player)** | |

| | White | Black | | White | Black | | White | Black |
|---|---|---|---|---|---|---|---|---|
| 1 | | | 21 | | | 41 | | |
| 2 | | | 22 | | | 42 | | |
| 3 | | | 23 | | | 43 | | |
| 4 | | | 24 | | | 44 | | |
| 5 | | | 25 | | | 45 | | |
| 6 | | | 26 | | | 46 | | |
| 7 | | | 27 | | | 47 | | |
| 8 | | | 28 | | | 48 | | |
| 9 | | | 29 | | | 49 | | |
| 10 | | | 30 | | | 50 | | |
| 11 | | | 31 | | | 51 | | |
| 12 | | | 32 | | | 52 | | |
| 13 | | | 33 | | | 53 | | |
| 14 | | | 34 | | | 54 | | |
| 15 | | | 35 | | | 55 | | |
| 16 | | | 36 | | | 56 | | |
| 17 | | | 37 | | | 57 | | |
| 18 | | | 38 | | | 58 | | |
| 19 | | | 39 | | | 59 | | |
| 20 | | | 40 | | | 60 | | |

## RESULTS

___ WHITE WON        ___ DRAW        ___ BLACK WON

Notes

8
7
6
5
4
3
2
1
A B C D E F G H

| SIGNATURE | | SIGNATURE | |
|---|---|---|---|

# SCORE SHEET

| EVENT | | DATE | |
|---|---|---|---|
| ROUND | | BOARD | |
| SECTION | | OPENING | |
| **WHITE (name of player)** | | **BLACK (name of player)** | |

| | White | Black | | White | Black | | White | Black |
|---|---|---|---|---|---|---|---|---|
| 1 | | | 21 | | | 41 | | |
| 2 | | | 22 | | | 42 | | |
| 3 | | | 23 | | | 43 | | |
| 4 | | | 24 | | | 44 | | |
| 5 | | | 25 | | | 45 | | |
| 6 | | | 26 | | | 46 | | |
| 7 | | | 27 | | | 47 | | |
| 8 | | | 28 | | | 48 | | |
| 9 | | | 29 | | | 49 | | |
| 10 | | | 30 | | | 50 | | |
| 11 | | | 31 | | | 51 | | |
| 12 | | | 32 | | | 52 | | |
| 13 | | | 33 | | | 53 | | |
| 14 | | | 34 | | | 54 | | |
| 15 | | | 35 | | | 55 | | |
| 16 | | | 36 | | | 56 | | |
| 17 | | | 37 | | | 57 | | |
| 18 | | | 38 | | | 58 | | |
| 19 | | | 39 | | | 59 | | |
| 20 | | | 40 | | | 60 | | |

## RESULTS

___ WHITE WON          ___ DRAW          ___ BLACK WON

| Notes |
|---|
| |
| |
| |
| |
| |
| |
| |
| |

| SIGNATURE | | SIGNATURE | |
|---|---|---|---|

# SCORE SHEET

| EVENT | | DATE | |
|---|---|---|---|
| ROUND | | BOARD | |
| SECTION | | OPENING | |
| **WHITE (name of player)** | | **BLACK (name of player)** | |

| | White | Black | | White | Black | | White | Black |
|---|---|---|---|---|---|---|---|---|
| 1 | | | 21 | | | 41 | | |
| 2 | | | 22 | | | 42 | | |
| 3 | | | 23 | | | 43 | | |
| 4 | | | 24 | | | 44 | | |
| 5 | | | 25 | | | 45 | | |
| 6 | | | 26 | | | 46 | | |
| 7 | | | 27 | | | 47 | | |
| 8 | | | 28 | | | 48 | | |
| 9 | | | 29 | | | 49 | | |
| 10 | | | 30 | | | 50 | | |
| 11 | | | 31 | | | 51 | | |
| 12 | | | 32 | | | 52 | | |
| 13 | | | 33 | | | 53 | | |
| 14 | | | 34 | | | 54 | | |
| 15 | | | 35 | | | 55 | | |
| 16 | | | 36 | | | 56 | | |
| 17 | | | 37 | | | 57 | | |
| 18 | | | 38 | | | 58 | | |
| 19 | | | 39 | | | 59 | | |
| 20 | | | 40 | | | 60 | | |

## RESULTS

___ WHITE WON          ___ DRAW          ___ BLACK WON

Notes

SIGNATURE                    SIGNATURE

# SCORE SHEET

| EVENT | | DATE | |
|---|---|---|---|
| ROUND | | BOARD | |
| SECTION | | OPENING | |
| **WHITE (name of player)** | | **BLACK (name of player)** | |

| | White | Black | | White | Black | | White | Black |
|---|---|---|---|---|---|---|---|---|
| 1 | | | 21 | | | 41 | | |
| 2 | | | 22 | | | 42 | | |
| 3 | | | 23 | | | 43 | | |
| 4 | | | 24 | | | 44 | | |
| 5 | | | 25 | | | 45 | | |
| 6 | | | 26 | | | 46 | | |
| 7 | | | 27 | | | 47 | | |
| 8 | | | 28 | | | 48 | | |
| 9 | | | 29 | | | 49 | | |
| 10 | | | 30 | | | 50 | | |
| 11 | | | 31 | | | 51 | | |
| 12 | | | 32 | | | 52 | | |
| 13 | | | 33 | | | 53 | | |
| 14 | | | 34 | | | 54 | | |
| 15 | | | 35 | | | 55 | | |
| 16 | | | 36 | | | 56 | | |
| 17 | | | 37 | | | 57 | | |
| 18 | | | 38 | | | 58 | | |
| 19 | | | 39 | | | 59 | | |
| 20 | | | 40 | | | 60 | | |

## RESULTS

___ WHITE WON          ___ DRAW          ___ BLACK WON

Notes

SIGNATURE

SIGNATURE

# SCORE SHEET

| EVENT | DATE |
|---|---|
| ROUND | BOARD |
| SECTION | OPENING |
| **WHITE (name of player)** | **BLACK (name of player)** |

| | White | Black | | White | Black | | White | Black |
|---|---|---|---|---|---|---|---|---|
| 1 | | | 21 | | | 41 | | |
| 2 | | | 22 | | | 42 | | |
| 3 | | | 23 | | | 43 | | |
| 4 | | | 24 | | | 44 | | |
| 5 | | | 25 | | | 45 | | |
| 6 | | | 26 | | | 46 | | |
| 7 | | | 27 | | | 47 | | |
| 8 | | | 28 | | | 48 | | |
| 9 | | | 29 | | | 49 | | |
| 10 | | | 30 | | | 50 | | |
| 11 | | | 31 | | | 51 | | |
| 12 | | | 32 | | | 52 | | |
| 13 | | | 33 | | | 53 | | |
| 14 | | | 34 | | | 54 | | |
| 15 | | | 35 | | | 55 | | |
| 16 | | | 36 | | | 56 | | |
| 17 | | | 37 | | | 57 | | |
| 18 | | | 38 | | | 58 | | |
| 19 | | | 39 | | | 59 | | |
| 20 | | | 40 | | | 60 | | |

## RESULTS

___ WHITE WON       ___ DRAW       ___ BLACK WON

Notes

| SIGNATURE | SIGNATURE |
|---|---|

# SCORE SHEET

| EVENT | | DATE | |
|---|---|---|---|
| ROUND | | BOARD | |
| SECTION | | OPENING | |
| **WHITE (name of player)** | | **BLACK (name of player)** | |

| | White | Black | | White | Black | | White | Black |
|---|---|---|---|---|---|---|---|---|
| 1 | | | 21 | | | 41 | | |
| 2 | | | 22 | | | 42 | | |
| 3 | | | 23 | | | 43 | | |
| 4 | | | 24 | | | 44 | | |
| 5 | | | 25 | | | 45 | | |
| 6 | | | 26 | | | 46 | | |
| 7 | | | 27 | | | 47 | | |
| 8 | | | 28 | | | 48 | | |
| 9 | | | 29 | | | 49 | | |
| 10 | | | 30 | | | 50 | | |
| 11 | | | 31 | | | 51 | | |
| 12 | | | 32 | | | 52 | | |
| 13 | | | 33 | | | 53 | | |
| 14 | | | 34 | | | 54 | | |
| 15 | | | 35 | | | 55 | | |
| 16 | | | 36 | | | 56 | | |
| 17 | | | 37 | | | 57 | | |
| 18 | | | 38 | | | 58 | | |
| 19 | | | 39 | | | 59 | | |
| 20 | | | 40 | | | 60 | | |

## RESULTS

___ WHITE WON          ___ DRAW          ___ BLACK WON

Notes

| SIGNATURE | SIGNATURE |
|---|---|

# SCORE SHEET

| EVENT | | DATE | |
|---|---|---|---|
| ROUND | | BOARD | |
| SECTION | | OPENING | |
| **WHITE (name of player)** | | **BLACK (name of player)** | |

| | White | Black | | White | Black | | White | Black |
|---|---|---|---|---|---|---|---|---|
| 1 | | | 21 | | | 41 | | |
| 2 | | | 22 | | | 42 | | |
| 3 | | | 23 | | | 43 | | |
| 4 | | | 24 | | | 44 | | |
| 5 | | | 25 | | | 45 | | |
| 6 | | | 26 | | | 46 | | |
| 7 | | | 27 | | | 47 | | |
| 8 | | | 28 | | | 48 | | |
| 9 | | | 29 | | | 49 | | |
| 10 | | | 30 | | | 50 | | |
| 11 | | | 31 | | | 51 | | |
| 12 | | | 32 | | | 52 | | |
| 13 | | | 33 | | | 53 | | |
| 14 | | | 34 | | | 54 | | |
| 15 | | | 35 | | | 55 | | |
| 16 | | | 36 | | | 56 | | |
| 17 | | | 37 | | | 57 | | |
| 18 | | | 38 | | | 58 | | |
| 19 | | | 39 | | | 59 | | |
| 20 | | | 40 | | | 60 | | |

## RESULTS

___ WHITE WON          ___ DRAW          ___ BLACK WON

Notes

SIGNATURE                    SIGNATURE

# SCORE SHEET

| EVENT | | DATE |
|---|---|---|
| ROUND | | BOARD |
| SECTION | | OPENING |
| **WHITE (name of player)** | | **BLACK (name of player)** |

| | White | Black | | White | Black | | White | Black |
|---|---|---|---|---|---|---|---|---|
| 1 | | | 21 | | | 41 | | |
| 2 | | | 22 | | | 42 | | |
| 3 | | | 23 | | | 43 | | |
| 4 | | | 24 | | | 44 | | |
| 5 | | | 25 | | | 45 | | |
| 6 | | | 26 | | | 46 | | |
| 7 | | | 27 | | | 47 | | |
| 8 | | | 28 | | | 48 | | |
| 9 | | | 29 | | | 49 | | |
| 10 | | | 30 | | | 50 | | |
| 11 | | | 31 | | | 51 | | |
| 12 | | | 32 | | | 52 | | |
| 13 | | | 33 | | | 53 | | |
| 14 | | | 34 | | | 54 | | |
| 15 | | | 35 | | | 55 | | |
| 16 | | | 36 | | | 56 | | |
| 17 | | | 37 | | | 57 | | |
| 18 | | | 38 | | | 58 | | |
| 19 | | | 39 | | | 59 | | |
| 20 | | | 40 | | | 60 | | |

## RESULTS

___ WHITE WON          ___ DRAW          ___ BLACK WON

8
7
6
5
4
3
2
1
A B C D E F G H

Notes

| SIGNATURE | | SIGNATURE |
|---|---|---|

# SCORE SHEET

| EVENT | DATE |
|---|---|
| ROUND | BOARD |
| SECTION | OPENING |
| **WHITE (name of player)** | **BLACK (name of player)** |

| | White | Black | | White | Black | | White | Black |
|---|---|---|---|---|---|---|---|---|
| 1 | | | 21 | | | 41 | | |
| 2 | | | 22 | | | 42 | | |
| 3 | | | 23 | | | 43 | | |
| 4 | | | 24 | | | 44 | | |
| 5 | | | 25 | | | 45 | | |
| 6 | | | 26 | | | 46 | | |
| 7 | | | 27 | | | 47 | | |
| 8 | | | 28 | | | 48 | | |
| 9 | | | 29 | | | 49 | | |
| 10 | | | 30 | | | 50 | | |
| 11 | | | 31 | | | 51 | | |
| 12 | | | 32 | | | 52 | | |
| 13 | | | 33 | | | 53 | | |
| 14 | | | 34 | | | 54 | | |
| 15 | | | 35 | | | 55 | | |
| 16 | | | 36 | | | 56 | | |
| 17 | | | 37 | | | 57 | | |
| 18 | | | 38 | | | 58 | | |
| 19 | | | 39 | | | 59 | | |
| 20 | | | 40 | | | 60 | | |

## RESULTS

___ WHITE WON          ___ DRAW          ___ BLACK WON

Notes

SIGNATURE                    SIGNATURE

# SCORE SHEET

| EVENT | | DATE | |
|---|---|---|---|
| ROUND | | BOARD | |
| SECTION | | OPENING | |
| **WHITE (name of player)** | | **BLACK (name of player)** | |

| | White | Black | | White | Black | | White | Black |
|---|---|---|---|---|---|---|---|---|
| 1 | | | 21 | | | 41 | | |
| 2 | | | 22 | | | 42 | | |
| 3 | | | 23 | | | 43 | | |
| 4 | | | 24 | | | 44 | | |
| 5 | | | 25 | | | 45 | | |
| 6 | | | 26 | | | 46 | | |
| 7 | | | 27 | | | 47 | | |
| 8 | | | 28 | | | 48 | | |
| 9 | | | 29 | | | 49 | | |
| 10 | | | 30 | | | 50 | | |
| 11 | | | 31 | | | 51 | | |
| 12 | | | 32 | | | 52 | | |
| 13 | | | 33 | | | 53 | | |
| 14 | | | 34 | | | 54 | | |
| 15 | | | 35 | | | 55 | | |
| 16 | | | 36 | | | 56 | | |
| 17 | | | 37 | | | 57 | | |
| 18 | | | 38 | | | 58 | | |
| 19 | | | 39 | | | 59 | | |
| 20 | | | 40 | | | 60 | | |

## RESULTS

___ WHITE WON  ___ DRAW  ___ BLACK WON

Notes

| SIGNATURE | SIGNATURE |
|---|---|

# SCORE SHEET

| EVENT | | DATE | |
|---|---|---|---|
| ROUND | | BOARD | |
| SECTION | | OPENING | |
| **WHITE (name of player)** | | **BLACK (name of player)** | |

| | White | Black | | White | Black | | White | Black |
|---|---|---|---|---|---|---|---|---|
| 1 | | | 21 | | | 41 | | |
| 2 | | | 22 | | | 42 | | |
| 3 | | | 23 | | | 43 | | |
| 4 | | | 24 | | | 44 | | |
| 5 | | | 25 | | | 45 | | |
| 6 | | | 26 | | | 46 | | |
| 7 | | | 27 | | | 47 | | |
| 8 | | | 28 | | | 48 | | |
| 9 | | | 29 | | | 49 | | |
| 10 | | | 30 | | | 50 | | |
| 11 | | | 31 | | | 51 | | |
| 12 | | | 32 | | | 52 | | |
| 13 | | | 33 | | | 53 | | |
| 14 | | | 34 | | | 54 | | |
| 15 | | | 35 | | | 55 | | |
| 16 | | | 36 | | | 56 | | |
| 17 | | | 37 | | | 57 | | |
| 18 | | | 38 | | | 58 | | |
| 19 | | | 39 | | | 59 | | |
| 20 | | | 40 | | | 60 | | |

## RESULTS

___ WHITE WON          ___ DRAW          ___ BLACK WON

Notes

SIGNATURE                    SIGNATURE

# SCORE SHEET

| EVENT | | DATE | |
|---|---|---|---|
| ROUND | | BOARD | |
| SECTION | | OPENING | |
| **WHITE (name of player)** | | **BLACK (name of player)** | |

| | White | Black | | White | Black | | White | Black |
|---|---|---|---|---|---|---|---|---|
| 1 | | | 21 | | | 41 | | |
| 2 | | | 22 | | | 42 | | |
| 3 | | | 23 | | | 43 | | |
| 4 | | | 24 | | | 44 | | |
| 5 | | | 25 | | | 45 | | |
| 6 | | | 26 | | | 46 | | |
| 7 | | | 27 | | | 47 | | |
| 8 | | | 28 | | | 48 | | |
| 9 | | | 29 | | | 49 | | |
| 10 | | | 30 | | | 50 | | |
| 11 | | | 31 | | | 51 | | |
| 12 | | | 32 | | | 52 | | |
| 13 | | | 33 | | | 53 | | |
| 14 | | | 34 | | | 54 | | |
| 15 | | | 35 | | | 55 | | |
| 16 | | | 36 | | | 56 | | |
| 17 | | | 37 | | | 57 | | |
| 18 | | | 38 | | | 58 | | |
| 19 | | | 39 | | | 59 | | |
| 20 | | | 40 | | | 60 | | |

## RESULTS

___ WHITE WON          ___ DRAW          ___ BLACK WON

Notes

SIGNATURE                    SIGNATURE

# SCORE SHEET

| EVENT | DATE |
|---|---|
| ROUND | BOARD |
| SECTION | OPENING |
| **WHITE (name of player)** | **BLACK (name of player)** |

| | White | Black | | White | Black | | White | Black |
|---|---|---|---|---|---|---|---|---|
| 1 | | | 21 | | | 41 | | |
| 2 | | | 22 | | | 42 | | |
| 3 | | | 23 | | | 43 | | |
| 4 | | | 24 | | | 44 | | |
| 5 | | | 25 | | | 45 | | |
| 6 | | | 26 | | | 46 | | |
| 7 | | | 27 | | | 47 | | |
| 8 | | | 28 | | | 48 | | |
| 9 | | | 29 | | | 49 | | |
| 10 | | | 30 | | | 50 | | |
| 11 | | | 31 | | | 51 | | |
| 12 | | | 32 | | | 52 | | |
| 13 | | | 33 | | | 53 | | |
| 14 | | | 34 | | | 54 | | |
| 15 | | | 35 | | | 55 | | |
| 16 | | | 36 | | | 56 | | |
| 17 | | | 37 | | | 57 | | |
| 18 | | | 38 | | | 58 | | |
| 19 | | | 39 | | | 59 | | |
| 20 | | | 40 | | | 60 | | |

## RESULTS

___ WHITE WON          ___ DRAW          ___ BLACK WON

Notes

| SIGNATURE | SIGNATURE |
|---|---|

# SCORE SHEET

| | |
|---|---|
| EVENT | DATE |
| ROUND | BOARD |
| SECTION | OPENING |
| **WHITE (name of player)** | **BLACK (name of player)** |

| | White | Black | | White | Black | | White | Black |
|---|---|---|---|---|---|---|---|---|
| 1 | | | 21 | | | 41 | | |
| 2 | | | 22 | | | 42 | | |
| 3 | | | 23 | | | 43 | | |
| 4 | | | 24 | | | 44 | | |
| 5 | | | 25 | | | 45 | | |
| 6 | | | 26 | | | 46 | | |
| 7 | | | 27 | | | 47 | | |
| 8 | | | 28 | | | 48 | | |
| 9 | | | 29 | | | 49 | | |
| 10 | | | 30 | | | 50 | | |
| 11 | | | 31 | | | 51 | | |
| 12 | | | 32 | | | 52 | | |
| 13 | | | 33 | | | 53 | | |
| 14 | | | 34 | | | 54 | | |
| 15 | | | 35 | | | 55 | | |
| 16 | | | 36 | | | 56 | | |
| 17 | | | 37 | | | 57 | | |
| 18 | | | 38 | | | 58 | | |
| 19 | | | 39 | | | 59 | | |
| 20 | | | 40 | | | 60 | | |

**RESULTS**

___ WHITE WON ___ DRAW ___ BLACK WON

8 7 6 5 4 3 2 1

A B C D E F G H

Notes

SIGNATURE SIGNATURE

# SCORE SHEET

| EVENT | DATE |
|---|---|
| ROUND | BOARD |
| SECTION | OPENING |
| **WHITE (name of player)** | **BLACK (name of player)** |

| | White | Black | | White | Black | | White | Black |
|---|---|---|---|---|---|---|---|---|
| 1 | | | 21 | | | 41 | | |
| 2 | | | 22 | | | 42 | | |
| 3 | | | 23 | | | 43 | | |
| 4 | | | 24 | | | 44 | | |
| 5 | | | 25 | | | 45 | | |
| 6 | | | 26 | | | 46 | | |
| 7 | | | 27 | | | 47 | | |
| 8 | | | 28 | | | 48 | | |
| 9 | | | 29 | | | 49 | | |
| 10 | | | 30 | | | 50 | | |
| 11 | | | 31 | | | 51 | | |
| 12 | | | 32 | | | 52 | | |
| 13 | | | 33 | | | 53 | | |
| 14 | | | 34 | | | 54 | | |
| 15 | | | 35 | | | 55 | | |
| 16 | | | 36 | | | 56 | | |
| 17 | | | 37 | | | 57 | | |
| 18 | | | 38 | | | 58 | | |
| 19 | | | 39 | | | 59 | | |
| 20 | | | 40 | | | 60 | | |

## RESULTS

___ WHITE WON        ___ DRAW        ___ BLACK WON

Notes

SIGNATURE                SIGNATURE

# SCORE SHEET

| EVENT | DATE |
|---|---|
| ROUND | BOARD |
| SECTION | OPENING |
| **WHITE (name of player)** | **BLACK (name of player)** |

| | White | Black | | White | Black | | White | Black |
|---|---|---|---|---|---|---|---|---|
| 1 | | | 21 | | | 41 | | |
| 2 | | | 22 | | | 42 | | |
| 3 | | | 23 | | | 43 | | |
| 4 | | | 24 | | | 44 | | |
| 5 | | | 25 | | | 45 | | |
| 6 | | | 26 | | | 46 | | |
| 7 | | | 27 | | | 47 | | |
| 8 | | | 28 | | | 48 | | |
| 9 | | | 29 | | | 49 | | |
| 10 | | | 30 | | | 50 | | |
| 11 | | | 31 | | | 51 | | |
| 12 | | | 32 | | | 52 | | |
| 13 | | | 33 | | | 53 | | |
| 14 | | | 34 | | | 54 | | |
| 15 | | | 35 | | | 55 | | |
| 16 | | | 36 | | | 56 | | |
| 17 | | | 37 | | | 57 | | |
| 18 | | | 38 | | | 58 | | |
| 19 | | | 39 | | | 59 | | |
| 20 | | | 40 | | | 60 | | |

## RESULTS

___ WHITE WON          ___ DRAW          ___ BLACK WON

Notes

SIGNATURE                    SIGNATURE

# SCORE SHEET

| EVENT | DATE |
|---|---|
| ROUND | BOARD |
| SECTION | OPENING |
| **WHITE (name of player)** | **BLACK (name of player)** |

| | White | Black | | White | Black | | White | Black |
|---|---|---|---|---|---|---|---|---|
| 1 | | | 21 | | | 41 | | |
| 2 | | | 22 | | | 42 | | |
| 3 | | | 23 | | | 43 | | |
| 4 | | | 24 | | | 44 | | |
| 5 | | | 25 | | | 45 | | |
| 6 | | | 26 | | | 46 | | |
| 7 | | | 27 | | | 47 | | |
| 8 | | | 28 | | | 48 | | |
| 9 | | | 29 | | | 49 | | |
| 10 | | | 30 | | | 50 | | |
| 11 | | | 31 | | | 51 | | |
| 12 | | | 32 | | | 52 | | |
| 13 | | | 33 | | | 53 | | |
| 14 | | | 34 | | | 54 | | |
| 15 | | | 35 | | | 55 | | |
| 16 | | | 36 | | | 56 | | |
| 17 | | | 37 | | | 57 | | |
| 18 | | | 38 | | | 58 | | |
| 19 | | | 39 | | | 59 | | |
| 20 | | | 40 | | | 60 | | |

## RESULTS

___ WHITE WON          ___ DRAW          ___ BLACK WON

Notes

| SIGNATURE | SIGNATURE |
|---|---|

# SCORE SHEET

| EVENT | DATE |
|---|---|
| ROUND | BOARD |
| SECTION | OPENING |
| **WHITE (name of player)** | **BLACK (name of player)** |

| | White | Black | | White | Black | | White | Black |
|---|---|---|---|---|---|---|---|---|
| 1 | | | 21 | | | 41 | | |
| 2 | | | 22 | | | 42 | | |
| 3 | | | 23 | | | 43 | | |
| 4 | | | 24 | | | 44 | | |
| 5 | | | 25 | | | 45 | | |
| 6 | | | 26 | | | 46 | | |
| 7 | | | 27 | | | 47 | | |
| 8 | | | 28 | | | 48 | | |
| 9 | | | 29 | | | 49 | | |
| 10 | | | 30 | | | 50 | | |
| 11 | | | 31 | | | 51 | | |
| 12 | | | 32 | | | 52 | | |
| 13 | | | 33 | | | 53 | | |
| 14 | | | 34 | | | 54 | | |
| 15 | | | 35 | | | 55 | | |
| 16 | | | 36 | | | 56 | | |
| 17 | | | 37 | | | 57 | | |
| 18 | | | 38 | | | 58 | | |
| 19 | | | 39 | | | 59 | | |
| 20 | | | 40 | | | 60 | | |

## RESULTS

___ WHITE WON          ___ DRAW          ___ BLACK WON

Notes

| SIGNATURE | SIGNATURE |
|---|---|

# SCORE SHEET

| EVENT | | DATE | |
| SECTION | | BOARD | |
| ROUND | | OPENING | |
| **WHITE (name of player)** | | **BLACK (name of player)** | |

| | White | Black | | White | Black | | White | Black |
|---|---|---|---|---|---|---|---|---|
| 1 | | | 21 | | | 41 | | |
| 2 | | | 22 | | | 42 | | |
| 3 | | | 23 | | | 43 | | |
| 4 | | | 24 | | | 44 | | |
| 5 | | | 25 | | | 45 | | |
| 6 | | | 26 | | | 46 | | |
| 7 | | | 27 | | | 47 | | |
| 8 | | | 28 | | | 48 | | |
| 9 | | | 29 | | | 49 | | |
| 10 | | | 30 | | | 50 | | |
| 11 | | | 31 | | | 51 | | |
| 12 | | | 32 | | | 52 | | |
| 13 | | | 33 | | | 53 | | |
| 14 | | | 34 | | | 54 | | |
| 15 | | | 35 | | | 55 | | |
| 16 | | | 36 | | | 56 | | |
| 17 | | | 37 | | | 57 | | |
| 18 | | | 38 | | | 58 | | |
| 19 | | | 39 | | | 59 | | |
| 20 | | | 40 | | | 60 | | |

## RESULTS

___ WHITE WON          ___ DRAW          ___ BLACK WON

Notes

SIGNATURE                              SIGNATURE

# SCORE SHEET

| EVENT | | DATE | |
| ROUND | | BOARD | |
| SECTION | | OPENING | |
| **WHITE (name of player)** | | **BLACK (name of player)** | |

| | White | Black | | White | Black | | White | Black |
|---|---|---|---|---|---|---|---|---|
| 1 | | | 21 | | | 41 | | |
| 2 | | | 22 | | | 42 | | |
| 3 | | | 23 | | | 43 | | |
| 4 | | | 24 | | | 44 | | |
| 5 | | | 25 | | | 45 | | |
| 6 | | | 26 | | | 46 | | |
| 7 | | | 27 | | | 47 | | |
| 8 | | | 28 | | | 48 | | |
| 9 | | | 29 | | | 49 | | |
| 10 | | | 30 | | | 50 | | |
| 11 | | | 31 | | | 51 | | |
| 12 | | | 32 | | | 52 | | |
| 13 | | | 33 | | | 53 | | |
| 14 | | | 34 | | | 54 | | |
| 15 | | | 35 | | | 55 | | |
| 16 | | | 36 | | | 56 | | |
| 17 | | | 37 | | | 57 | | |
| 18 | | | 38 | | | 58 | | |
| 19 | | | 39 | | | 59 | | |
| 20 | | | 40 | | | 60 | | |

## RESULTS

___ WHITE WON          ___ DRAW          ___ BLACK WON

Notes

| SIGNATURE | | SIGNATURE | |

# SCORE SHEET

| EVENT | | DATE | |
|---|---|---|---|
| ROUND | | BOARD | |
| SECTION | | OPENING | |
| **WHITE (name of player)** | | **BLACK (name of player)** | |

| | White | Black | | White | Black | | White | Black |
|---|---|---|---|---|---|---|---|---|
| 1 | | | 21 | | | 41 | | |
| 2 | | | 22 | | | 42 | | |
| 3 | | | 23 | | | 43 | | |
| 4 | | | 24 | | | 44 | | |
| 5 | | | 25 | | | 45 | | |
| 6 | | | 26 | | | 46 | | |
| 7 | | | 27 | | | 47 | | |
| 8 | | | 28 | | | 48 | | |
| 9 | | | 29 | | | 49 | | |
| 10 | | | 30 | | | 50 | | |
| 11 | | | 31 | | | 51 | | |
| 12 | | | 32 | | | 52 | | |
| 13 | | | 33 | | | 53 | | |
| 14 | | | 34 | | | 54 | | |
| 15 | | | 35 | | | 55 | | |
| 16 | | | 36 | | | 56 | | |
| 17 | | | 37 | | | 57 | | |
| 18 | | | 38 | | | 58 | | |
| 19 | | | 39 | | | 59 | | |
| 20 | | | 40 | | | 60 | | |

## RESULTS

___ WHITE WON          ___ DRAW          ___ BLACK WON

Notes

| SIGNATURE | SIGNATURE |

# SCORE SHEET

| EVENT | DATE |
|---|---|
| ROUND | BOARD |
| SECTION | OPENING |
| **WHITE (name of player)** | **BLACK (name of player)** |

| | White | Black | | White | Black | | White | Black |
|---|---|---|---|---|---|---|---|---|
| 1 | | | 21 | | | 41 | | |
| 2 | | | 22 | | | 42 | | |
| 3 | | | 23 | | | 43 | | |
| 4 | | | 24 | | | 44 | | |
| 5 | | | 25 | | | 45 | | |
| 6 | | | 26 | | | 46 | | |
| 7 | | | 27 | | | 47 | | |
| 8 | | | 28 | | | 48 | | |
| 9 | | | 29 | | | 49 | | |
| 10 | | | 30 | | | 50 | | |
| 11 | | | 31 | | | 51 | | |
| 12 | | | 32 | | | 52 | | |
| 13 | | | 33 | | | 53 | | |
| 14 | | | 34 | | | 54 | | |
| 15 | | | 35 | | | 55 | | |
| 16 | | | 36 | | | 56 | | |
| 17 | | | 37 | | | 57 | | |
| 18 | | | 38 | | | 58 | | |
| 19 | | | 39 | | | 59 | | |
| 20 | | | 40 | | | 60 | | |

## RESULTS

___ WHITE WON        ___ DRAW        ___ BLACK WON

| | Notes |
|---|---|
| 8 7 6 5 4 3 2 1 A B C D E F G H | |

| SIGNATURE | SIGNATURE |
|---|---|

# SCORE SHEET

| EVENT | | DATE | |
|---|---|---|---|
| ROUND | | BOARD | |
| SECTION | | OPENING | |
| **WHITE (name of player)** | | **BLACK (name of player)** | |

| | White | Black | | White | Black | | White | Black |
|---|---|---|---|---|---|---|---|---|
| 1 | | | 21 | | | 41 | | |
| 2 | | | 22 | | | 42 | | |
| 3 | | | 23 | | | 43 | | |
| 4 | | | 24 | | | 44 | | |
| 5 | | | 25 | | | 45 | | |
| 6 | | | 26 | | | 46 | | |
| 7 | | | 27 | | | 47 | | |
| 8 | | | 28 | | | 48 | | |
| 9 | | | 29 | | | 49 | | |
| 10 | | | 30 | | | 50 | | |
| 11 | | | 31 | | | 51 | | |
| 12 | | | 32 | | | 52 | | |
| 13 | | | 33 | | | 53 | | |
| 14 | | | 34 | | | 54 | | |
| 15 | | | 35 | | | 55 | | |
| 16 | | | 36 | | | 56 | | |
| 17 | | | 37 | | | 57 | | |
| 18 | | | 38 | | | 58 | | |
| 19 | | | 39 | | | 59 | | |
| 20 | | | 40 | | | 60 | | |

## RESULTS

___ WHITE WON          ___ DRAW          ___ BLACK WON

Notes

| SIGNATURE | | SIGNATURE | |

# SCORE SHEET

| EVENT | | DATE | |
| --- | --- | --- | --- |
| ROUND | | BOARD | |
| SECTION | | OPENING | |
| **WHITE (name of player)** | | **BLACK (name of player)** | |

| | White | Black | | White | Black | | White | Black |
| --- | --- | --- | --- | --- | --- | --- | --- | --- |
| 1 | | | 21 | | | 41 | | |
| 2 | | | 22 | | | 42 | | |
| 3 | | | 23 | | | 43 | | |
| 4 | | | 24 | | | 44 | | |
| 5 | | | 25 | | | 45 | | |
| 6 | | | 26 | | | 46 | | |
| 7 | | | 27 | | | 47 | | |
| 8 | | | 28 | | | 48 | | |
| 9 | | | 29 | | | 49 | | |
| 10 | | | 30 | | | 50 | | |
| 11 | | | 31 | | | 51 | | |
| 12 | | | 32 | | | 52 | | |
| 13 | | | 33 | | | 53 | | |
| 14 | | | 34 | | | 54 | | |
| 15 | | | 35 | | | 55 | | |
| 16 | | | 36 | | | 56 | | |
| 17 | | | 37 | | | 57 | | |
| 18 | | | 38 | | | 58 | | |
| 19 | | | 39 | | | 59 | | |
| 20 | | | 40 | | | 60 | | |

## RESULTS

___ WHITE WON          ___ DRAW          ___ BLACK WON

Notes

SIGNATURE                          SIGNATURE

# SCORE SHEET

| EVENT | DATE |
|---|---|
| ROUND | BOARD |
| SECTION | OPENING |
| **WHITE (name of player)** | **BLACK (name of player)** |

| | White | Black | | White | Black | | White | Black |
|---|---|---|---|---|---|---|---|---|
| 1 | | | 21 | | | 41 | | |
| 2 | | | 22 | | | 42 | | |
| 3 | | | 23 | | | 43 | | |
| 4 | | | 24 | | | 44 | | |
| 5 | | | 25 | | | 45 | | |
| 6 | | | 26 | | | 46 | | |
| 7 | | | 27 | | | 47 | | |
| 8 | | | 28 | | | 48 | | |
| 9 | | | 29 | | | 49 | | |
| 10 | | | 30 | | | 50 | | |
| 11 | | | 31 | | | 51 | | |
| 12 | | | 32 | | | 52 | | |
| 13 | | | 33 | | | 53 | | |
| 14 | | | 34 | | | 54 | | |
| 15 | | | 35 | | | 55 | | |
| 16 | | | 36 | | | 56 | | |
| 17 | | | 37 | | | 57 | | |
| 18 | | | 38 | | | 58 | | |
| 19 | | | 39 | | | 59 | | |
| 20 | | | 40 | | | 60 | | |

## RESULTS

___ WHITE WON          ___ DRAW          ___ BLACK WON

Notes

| SIGNATURE | SIGNATURE |
|---|---|

# SCORE SHEET

| EVENT | DATE |
|---|---|
| ROUND | BOARD |
| SECTION | OPENING |
| **WHITE (name of player)** | **BLACK (name of player)** |

| | White | Black | | White | Black | | White | Black |
|---|---|---|---|---|---|---|---|---|
| 1 | | | 21 | | | 41 | | |
| 2 | | | 22 | | | 42 | | |
| 3 | | | 23 | | | 43 | | |
| 4 | | | 24 | | | 44 | | |
| 5 | | | 25 | | | 45 | | |
| 6 | | | 26 | | | 46 | | |
| 7 | | | 27 | | | 47 | | |
| 8 | | | 28 | | | 48 | | |
| 9 | | | 29 | | | 49 | | |
| 10 | | | 30 | | | 50 | | |
| 11 | | | 31 | | | 51 | | |
| 12 | | | 32 | | | 52 | | |
| 13 | | | 33 | | | 53 | | |
| 14 | | | 34 | | | 54 | | |
| 15 | | | 35 | | | 55 | | |
| 16 | | | 36 | | | 56 | | |
| 17 | | | 37 | | | 57 | | |
| 18 | | | 38 | | | 58 | | |
| 19 | | | 39 | | | 59 | | |
| 20 | | | 40 | | | 60 | | |

## RESULTS

___ WHITE WON          ___ DRAW          ___ BLACK WON

Notes

```
8
7
6
5
4
3
2
1
  A B C D E F G H
```

| SIGNATURE | SIGNATURE |
|---|---|

# SCORE SHEET

| EVENT | | DATE | |
|---|---|---|---|
| ROUND | | BOARD | |
| SECTION | | OPENING | |
| **WHITE (name of player)** | | **BLACK (name of player)** | |

| | White | Black | | White | Black | | White | Black |
|---|---|---|---|---|---|---|---|---|
| 1 | | | 21 | | | 41 | | |
| 2 | | | 22 | | | 42 | | |
| 3 | | | 23 | | | 43 | | |
| 4 | | | 24 | | | 44 | | |
| 5 | | | 25 | | | 45 | | |
| 6 | | | 26 | | | 46 | | |
| 7 | | | 27 | | | 47 | | |
| 8 | | | 28 | | | 48 | | |
| 9 | | | 29 | | | 49 | | |
| 10 | | | 30 | | | 50 | | |
| 11 | | | 31 | | | 51 | | |
| 12 | | | 32 | | | 52 | | |
| 13 | | | 33 | | | 53 | | |
| 14 | | | 34 | | | 54 | | |
| 15 | | | 35 | | | 55 | | |
| 16 | | | 36 | | | 56 | | |
| 17 | | | 37 | | | 57 | | |
| 18 | | | 38 | | | 58 | | |
| 19 | | | 39 | | | 59 | | |
| 20 | | | 40 | | | 60 | | |

## RESULTS

___ WHITE WON    ___ DRAW    ___ BLACK WON

Notes

8
7
6
5
4
3
2
1
A B C D E F G H

| SIGNATURE | | SIGNATURE | |
|---|---|---|---|

# SCORE SHEET

| EVENT | DATE |
|---|---|
| ROUND | BOARD |
| SECTION | OPENING |
| **WHITE (name of player)** | **BLACK (name of player)** |

| | White | Black | | White | Black | | White | Black |
|---|---|---|---|---|---|---|---|---|
| 1 | | | 21 | | | 41 | | |
| 2 | | | 22 | | | 42 | | |
| 3 | | | 23 | | | 43 | | |
| 4 | | | 24 | | | 44 | | |
| 5 | | | 25 | | | 45 | | |
| 6 | | | 26 | | | 46 | | |
| 7 | | | 27 | | | 47 | | |
| 8 | | | 28 | | | 48 | | |
| 9 | | | 29 | | | 49 | | |
| 10 | | | 30 | | | 50 | | |
| 11 | | | 31 | | | 51 | | |
| 12 | | | 32 | | | 52 | | |
| 13 | | | 33 | | | 53 | | |
| 14 | | | 34 | | | 54 | | |
| 15 | | | 35 | | | 55 | | |
| 16 | | | 36 | | | 56 | | |
| 17 | | | 37 | | | 57 | | |
| 18 | | | 38 | | | 58 | | |
| 19 | | | 39 | | | 59 | | |
| 20 | | | 40 | | | 60 | | |

## RESULTS

___ WHITE WON          ___ DRAW          ___ BLACK WON

Notes

SIGNATURE                    SIGNATURE

# SCORE SHEET

| EVENT | DATE |
|-------|------|
| ROUND | BOARD |
| SECTION | OPENING |
| **WHITE (name of player)** | **BLACK (name of player)** |

| | White | Black | | White | Black | | White | Black |
|----|-------|-------|----|-------|-------|----|-------|-------|
| 1 | | | 21 | | | 41 | | |
| 2 | | | 22 | | | 42 | | |
| 3 | | | 23 | | | 43 | | |
| 4 | | | 24 | | | 44 | | |
| 5 | | | 25 | | | 45 | | |
| 6 | | | 26 | | | 46 | | |
| 7 | | | 27 | | | 47 | | |
| 8 | | | 28 | | | 48 | | |
| 9 | | | 29 | | | 49 | | |
| 10 | | | 30 | | | 50 | | |
| 11 | | | 31 | | | 51 | | |
| 12 | | | 32 | | | 52 | | |
| 13 | | | 33 | | | 53 | | |
| 14 | | | 34 | | | 54 | | |
| 15 | | | 35 | | | 55 | | |
| 16 | | | 36 | | | 56 | | |
| 17 | | | 37 | | | 57 | | |
| 18 | | | 38 | | | 58 | | |
| 19 | | | 39 | | | 59 | | |
| 20 | | | 40 | | | 60 | | |

## RESULTS

___ WHITE WON          ___ DRAW          ___ BLACK WON

Notes

SIGNATURE                    SIGNATURE

# SCORE SHEET

| EVENT | | DATE | |
|---|---|---|---|
| ROUND | | BOARD | |
| SECTION | | OPENING | |
| **WHITE (name of player)** | | **BLACK (name of player)** | |

| | White | Black | | White | Black | | White | Black |
|---|---|---|---|---|---|---|---|---|
| 1 | | | 21 | | | 41 | | |
| 2 | | | 22 | | | 42 | | |
| 3 | | | 23 | | | 43 | | |
| 4 | | | 24 | | | 44 | | |
| 5 | | | 25 | | | 45 | | |
| 6 | | | 26 | | | 46 | | |
| 7 | | | 27 | | | 47 | | |
| 8 | | | 28 | | | 48 | | |
| 9 | | | 29 | | | 49 | | |
| 10 | | | 30 | | | 50 | | |
| 11 | | | 31 | | | 51 | | |
| 12 | | | 32 | | | 52 | | |
| 13 | | | 33 | | | 53 | | |
| 14 | | | 34 | | | 54 | | |
| 15 | | | 35 | | | 55 | | |
| 16 | | | 36 | | | 56 | | |
| 17 | | | 37 | | | 57 | | |
| 18 | | | 38 | | | 58 | | |
| 19 | | | 39 | | | 59 | | |
| 20 | | | 40 | | | 60 | | |

## RESULTS

___ WHITE WON     ___ DRAW     ___ BLACK WON

Notes

A B C D E F G H
8 7 6 5 4 3 2 1

| SIGNATURE | SIGNATURE |
|---|---|

# SCORE SHEET

| EVENT | | DATE | |
|---|---|---|---|
| ROUND | | BOARD | |
| SECTION | | OPENING | |
| **WHITE (name of player)** | | **BLACK (name of player)** | |

| | White | Black | | White | Black | | White | Black |
|---|---|---|---|---|---|---|---|---|
| 1 | | | 21 | | | 41 | | |
| 2 | | | 22 | | | 42 | | |
| 3 | | | 23 | | | 43 | | |
| 4 | | | 24 | | | 44 | | |
| 5 | | | 25 | | | 45 | | |
| 6 | | | 26 | | | 46 | | |
| 7 | | | 27 | | | 47 | | |
| 8 | | | 28 | | | 48 | | |
| 9 | | | 29 | | | 49 | | |
| 10 | | | 30 | | | 50 | | |
| 11 | | | 31 | | | 51 | | |
| 12 | | | 32 | | | 52 | | |
| 13 | | | 33 | | | 53 | | |
| 14 | | | 34 | | | 54 | | |
| 15 | | | 35 | | | 55 | | |
| 16 | | | 36 | | | 56 | | |
| 17 | | | 37 | | | 57 | | |
| 18 | | | 38 | | | 58 | | |
| 19 | | | 39 | | | 59 | | |
| 20 | | | 40 | | | 60 | | |

## RESULTS

___ WHITE WON          ___ DRAW          ___ BLACK WON

Notes

```
8 ■□■□■□■□
7 □■□■□■□■
6 ■□■□■□■□
5 □■□■□■□■
4 ■□■□■□■□
3 □■□■□■□■
2 ■□■□■□■□
1 □■□■□■□■
  A B C D E F G H
```

| SIGNATURE | | SIGNATURE | |
|---|---|---|---|

# SCORE SHEET

| EVENT | | DATE | |
| ROUND | | BOARD | |
| SECTION | | OPENING | |
| **WHITE (name of player)** | | **BLACK (name of player)** | |

| | White | Black | | White | Black | | White | Black |
|---|---|---|---|---|---|---|---|---|
| 1 | | | 21 | | | 41 | | |
| 2 | | | 22 | | | 42 | | |
| 3 | | | 23 | | | 43 | | |
| 4 | | | 24 | | | 44 | | |
| 5 | | | 25 | | | 45 | | |
| 6 | | | 26 | | | 46 | | |
| 7 | | | 27 | | | 47 | | |
| 8 | | | 28 | | | 48 | | |
| 9 | | | 29 | | | 49 | | |
| 10 | | | 30 | | | 50 | | |
| 11 | | | 31 | | | 51 | | |
| 12 | | | 32 | | | 52 | | |
| 13 | | | 33 | | | 53 | | |
| 14 | | | 34 | | | 54 | | |
| 15 | | | 35 | | | 55 | | |
| 16 | | | 36 | | | 56 | | |
| 17 | | | 37 | | | 57 | | |
| 18 | | | 38 | | | 58 | | |
| 19 | | | 39 | | | 59 | | |
| 20 | | | 40 | | | 60 | | |

## RESULTS

___ WHITE WON        ___ DRAW        ___ BLACK WON

Notes

```
8 ■□■□■□■□
7 □■□■□■□■
6 ■□■□■□■□
5 □■□■□■□■
4 ■□■□■□■□
3 □■□■□■□■
2 ■□■□■□■□
1 □■□■□■□■
  A B C D E F G H
```

| SIGNATURE | | SIGNATURE | |

# SCORE SHEET

| EVENT | | DATE | |
| --- | --- | --- | --- |
| ROUND | | BOARD | |
| SECTION | | OPENING | |
| **WHITE (name of player)** | | **BLACK (name of player)** | |

| | White | Black | | White | Black | | White | Black |
| --- | --- | --- | --- | --- | --- | --- | --- | --- |
| 1 | | | 21 | | | 41 | | |
| 2 | | | 22 | | | 42 | | |
| 3 | | | 23 | | | 43 | | |
| 4 | | | 24 | | | 44 | | |
| 5 | | | 25 | | | 45 | | |
| 6 | | | 26 | | | 46 | | |
| 7 | | | 27 | | | 47 | | |
| 8 | | | 28 | | | 48 | | |
| 9 | | | 29 | | | 49 | | |
| 10 | | | 30 | | | 50 | | |
| 11 | | | 31 | | | 51 | | |
| 12 | | | 32 | | | 52 | | |
| 13 | | | 33 | | | 53 | | |
| 14 | | | 34 | | | 54 | | |
| 15 | | | 35 | | | 55 | | |
| 16 | | | 36 | | | 56 | | |
| 17 | | | 37 | | | 57 | | |
| 18 | | | 38 | | | 58 | | |
| 19 | | | 39 | | | 59 | | |
| 20 | | | 40 | | | 60 | | |

## RESULTS

___ WHITE WON            ___ DRAW            ___ BLACK WON

Notes

| SIGNATURE | | SIGNATURE | |
| --- | --- | --- | --- |

# SCORE SHEET

| EVENT | DATE |
|---|---|
| ROUND | BOARD |
| SECTION | OPENING |
| **WHITE (name of player)** | **BLACK (name of player)** |

| | White | Black | | White | Black | | White | Black |
|---|---|---|---|---|---|---|---|---|
| 1 | | | 21 | | | 41 | | |
| 2 | | | 22 | | | 42 | | |
| 3 | | | 23 | | | 43 | | |
| 4 | | | 24 | | | 44 | | |
| 5 | | | 25 | | | 45 | | |
| 6 | | | 26 | | | 46 | | |
| 7 | | | 27 | | | 47 | | |
| 8 | | | 28 | | | 48 | | |
| 9 | | | 29 | | | 49 | | |
| 10 | | | 30 | | | 50 | | |
| 11 | | | 31 | | | 51 | | |
| 12 | | | 32 | | | 52 | | |
| 13 | | | 33 | | | 53 | | |
| 14 | | | 34 | | | 54 | | |
| 15 | | | 35 | | | 55 | | |
| 16 | | | 36 | | | 56 | | |
| 17 | | | 37 | | | 57 | | |
| 18 | | | 38 | | | 58 | | |
| 19 | | | 39 | | | 59 | | |
| 20 | | | 40 | | | 60 | | |

## RESULTS

___ WHITE WON          ___ DRAW          ___ BLACK WON

Notes

SIGNATURE                               SIGNATURE

# SCORE SHEET

| EVENT | | DATE | |
| SECTION | | BOARD | |
| SECTION | | OPENING | |
| WHITE (name of player) | | BLACK (name of player) | |

| | White | Black | | White | Black | | White | Black |
|---|---|---|---|---|---|---|---|---|
| 1 | | | 21 | | | 41 | | |
| 2 | | | 22 | | | 42 | | |
| 3 | | | 23 | | | 43 | | |
| 4 | | | 24 | | | 44 | | |
| 5 | | | 25 | | | 45 | | |
| 6 | | | 26 | | | 46 | | |
| 7 | | | 27 | | | 47 | | |
| 8 | | | 28 | | | 48 | | |
| 9 | | | 29 | | | 49 | | |
| 10 | | | 30 | | | 50 | | |
| 11 | | | 31 | | | 51 | | |
| 12 | | | 32 | | | 52 | | |
| 13 | | | 33 | | | 53 | | |
| 14 | | | 34 | | | 54 | | |
| 15 | | | 35 | | | 55 | | |
| 16 | | | 36 | | | 56 | | |
| 17 | | | 37 | | | 57 | | |
| 18 | | | 38 | | | 58 | | |
| 19 | | | 39 | | | 59 | | |
| 20 | | | 40 | | | 60 | | |

## RESULTS

___ WHITE WON          ___ DRAW          ___ BLACK WON

Notes

| SIGNATURE | | SIGNATURE | |

# SCORE SHEET

| EVENT | | DATE | |
| --- | --- | --- | --- |
| ROUND | | BOARD | |
| SECTION | | OPENING | |
| **WHITE (name of player)** | | **BLACK (name of player)** | |

| | White | Black | | White | Black | | White | Black |
| --- | --- | --- | --- | --- | --- | --- | --- | --- |
| 1 | | | 21 | | | 41 | | |
| 2 | | | 22 | | | 42 | | |
| 3 | | | 23 | | | 43 | | |
| 4 | | | 24 | | | 44 | | |
| 5 | | | 25 | | | 45 | | |
| 6 | | | 26 | | | 46 | | |
| 7 | | | 27 | | | 47 | | |
| 8 | | | 28 | | | 48 | | |
| 9 | | | 29 | | | 49 | | |
| 10 | | | 30 | | | 50 | | |
| 11 | | | 31 | | | 51 | | |
| 12 | | | 32 | | | 52 | | |
| 13 | | | 33 | | | 53 | | |
| 14 | | | 34 | | | 54 | | |
| 15 | | | 35 | | | 55 | | |
| 16 | | | 36 | | | 56 | | |
| 17 | | | 37 | | | 57 | | |
| 18 | | | 38 | | | 58 | | |
| 19 | | | 39 | | | 59 | | |
| 20 | | | 40 | | | 60 | | |

## RESULTS

___ WHITE WON          ___ DRAW          ___ BLACK WON

Notes

8
7
6
5
4
3
2
1
A B C D E F G H

| SIGNATURE | SIGNATURE |
| --- | --- |

# SCORE SHEET

| EVENT | DATE |
|---|---|
| ROUND | BOARD |
| SECTION | OPENING |
| **WHITE (name of player)** | **BLACK (name of player)** |

| | White | Black | | White | Black | | White | Black |
|---|---|---|---|---|---|---|---|---|
| 1 | | | 21 | | | 41 | | |
| 2 | | | 22 | | | 42 | | |
| 3 | | | 23 | | | 43 | | |
| 4 | | | 24 | | | 44 | | |
| 5 | | | 25 | | | 45 | | |
| 6 | | | 26 | | | 46 | | |
| 7 | | | 27 | | | 47 | | |
| 8 | | | 28 | | | 48 | | |
| 9 | | | 29 | | | 49 | | |
| 10 | | | 30 | | | 50 | | |
| 11 | | | 31 | | | 51 | | |
| 12 | | | 32 | | | 52 | | |
| 13 | | | 33 | | | 53 | | |
| 14 | | | 34 | | | 54 | | |
| 15 | | | 35 | | | 55 | | |
| 16 | | | 36 | | | 56 | | |
| 17 | | | 37 | | | 57 | | |
| 18 | | | 38 | | | 58 | | |
| 19 | | | 39 | | | 59 | | |
| 20 | | | 40 | | | 60 | | |

## RESULTS

___ WHITE WON        ___ DRAW        ___ BLACK WON

Notes

SIGNATURE                SIGNATURE

# SCORE SHEET

| EVENT | | DATE |
|---|---|---|
| ROUND | | BOARD |
| SECTION | | OPENING |
| **WHITE (name of player)** | | **BLACK (name of player)** |

| | White | Black | | White | Black | | White | Black |
|---|---|---|---|---|---|---|---|---|
| 1 | | | 21 | | | 41 | | |
| 2 | | | 22 | | | 42 | | |
| 3 | | | 23 | | | 43 | | |
| 4 | | | 24 | | | 44 | | |
| 5 | | | 25 | | | 45 | | |
| 6 | | | 26 | | | 46 | | |
| 7 | | | 27 | | | 47 | | |
| 8 | | | 28 | | | 48 | | |
| 9 | | | 29 | | | 49 | | |
| 10 | | | 30 | | | 50 | | |
| 11 | | | 31 | | | 51 | | |
| 12 | | | 32 | | | 52 | | |
| 13 | | | 33 | | | 53 | | |
| 14 | | | 34 | | | 54 | | |
| 15 | | | 35 | | | 55 | | |
| 16 | | | 36 | | | 56 | | |
| 17 | | | 37 | | | 57 | | |
| 18 | | | 38 | | | 58 | | |
| 19 | | | 39 | | | 59 | | |
| 20 | | | 40 | | | 60 | | |

## RESULTS

___ WHITE WON          ___ DRAW          ___ BLACK WON

Notes

SIGNATURE          SIGNATURE

# SCORE SHEET

| EVENT | | DATE | |
|---|---|---|---|
| ROUND | | BOARD | |
| SECTION | | OPENING | |
| **WHITE (name of player)** | | **BLACK (name of player)** | |

| | White | Black | | White | Black | | White | Black |
|---|---|---|---|---|---|---|---|---|
| 1 | | | 21 | | | 41 | | |
| 2 | | | 22 | | | 42 | | |
| 3 | | | 23 | | | 43 | | |
| 4 | | | 24 | | | 44 | | |
| 5 | | | 25 | | | 45 | | |
| 6 | | | 26 | | | 46 | | |
| 7 | | | 27 | | | 47 | | |
| 8 | | | 28 | | | 48 | | |
| 9 | | | 29 | | | 49 | | |
| 10 | | | 30 | | | 50 | | |
| 11 | | | 31 | | | 51 | | |
| 12 | | | 32 | | | 52 | | |
| 13 | | | 33 | | | 53 | | |
| 14 | | | 34 | | | 54 | | |
| 15 | | | 35 | | | 55 | | |
| 16 | | | 36 | | | 56 | | |
| 17 | | | 37 | | | 57 | | |
| 18 | | | 38 | | | 58 | | |
| 19 | | | 39 | | | 59 | | |
| 20 | | | 40 | | | 60 | | |

## RESULTS

___ WHITE WON          ___ DRAW          ___ BLACK WON

Notes

SIGNATURE                    SIGNATURE

# SCORE SHEET

| | | | | | | | | |
|---|---|---|---|---|---|---|---|---|
| EVENT | | | | DATE | | | | |
| ROUND | | | | BOARD | | | | |
| SECTION | | | | OPENING | | | | |
| **WHITE (name of player)** | | | | **BLACK (name of player)** | | | | |

| | White | Black | | White | Black | | White | Black |
|---|---|---|---|---|---|---|---|---|
| 1 | | | 21 | | | 41 | | |
| 2 | | | 22 | | | 42 | | |
| 3 | | | 23 | | | 43 | | |
| 4 | | | 24 | | | 44 | | |
| 5 | | | 25 | | | 45 | | |
| 6 | | | 26 | | | 46 | | |
| 7 | | | 27 | | | 47 | | |
| 8 | | | 28 | | | 48 | | |
| 9 | | | 29 | | | 49 | | |
| 10 | | | 30 | | | 50 | | |
| 11 | | | 31 | | | 51 | | |
| 12 | | | 32 | | | 52 | | |
| 13 | | | 33 | | | 53 | | |
| 14 | | | 34 | | | 54 | | |
| 15 | | | 35 | | | 55 | | |
| 16 | | | 36 | | | 56 | | |
| 17 | | | 37 | | | 57 | | |
| 18 | | | 38 | | | 58 | | |
| 19 | | | 39 | | | 59 | | |
| 20 | | | 40 | | | 60 | | |

## RESULTS

___ WHITE WON          ___ DRAW          ___ BLACK WON

Notes

SIGNATURE

SIGNATURE

# SCORE SHEET

| EVENT | | DATE | |
|---|---|---|---|
| ROUND | | BOARD | |
| SECTION | | OPENING | |
| **WHITE (name of player)** | | **BLACK (name of player)** | |

| | White | Black | | White | Black | | White | Black |
|---|---|---|---|---|---|---|---|---|
| 1 | | | 21 | | | 41 | | |
| 2 | | | 22 | | | 42 | | |
| 3 | | | 23 | | | 43 | | |
| 4 | | | 24 | | | 44 | | |
| 5 | | | 25 | | | 45 | | |
| 6 | | | 26 | | | 46 | | |
| 7 | | | 27 | | | 47 | | |
| 8 | | | 28 | | | 48 | | |
| 9 | | | 29 | | | 49 | | |
| 10 | | | 30 | | | 50 | | |
| 11 | | | 31 | | | 51 | | |
| 12 | | | 32 | | | 52 | | |
| 13 | | | 33 | | | 53 | | |
| 14 | | | 34 | | | 54 | | |
| 15 | | | 35 | | | 55 | | |
| 16 | | | 36 | | | 56 | | |
| 17 | | | 37 | | | 57 | | |
| 18 | | | 38 | | | 58 | | |
| 19 | | | 39 | | | 59 | | |
| 20 | | | 40 | | | 60 | | |

## RESULTS

___ WHITE WON          ___ DRAW          ___ BLACK WON

Notes

8
7
6
5
4
3
2
1
A B C D E F G H

| SIGNATURE | | SIGNATURE | |
|---|---|---|---|

# SCORE SHEET

| EVENT | | DATE | |
| ROUND | | BOARD | |
| SECTION | | OPENING | |

**WHITE (name of player)** | **BLACK (name of player)**

| | White | Black | | White | Black | | White | Black |
|---|---|---|---|---|---|---|---|---|
| 1 | | | 21 | | | 41 | | |
| 2 | | | 22 | | | 42 | | |
| 3 | | | 23 | | | 43 | | |
| 4 | | | 24 | | | 44 | | |
| 5 | | | 25 | | | 45 | | |
| 6 | | | 26 | | | 46 | | |
| 7 | | | 27 | | | 47 | | |
| 8 | | | 28 | | | 48 | | |
| 9 | | | 29 | | | 49 | | |
| 10 | | | 30 | | | 50 | | |
| 11 | | | 31 | | | 51 | | |
| 12 | | | 32 | | | 52 | | |
| 13 | | | 33 | | | 53 | | |
| 14 | | | 34 | | | 54 | | |
| 15 | | | 35 | | | 55 | | |
| 16 | | | 36 | | | 56 | | |
| 17 | | | 37 | | | 57 | | |
| 18 | | | 38 | | | 58 | | |
| 19 | | | 39 | | | 59 | | |
| 20 | | | 40 | | | 60 | | |

## RESULTS

___ WHITE WON        ___ DRAW        ___ BLACK WON

Notes

| SIGNATURE | | SIGNATURE | |

# SCORE SHEET

| EVENT | | DATE |
|---|---|---|
| ROUND | | BOARD |
| SECTION | | OPENING |
| **WHITE (name of player)** | | **BLACK (name of player)** |

| | White | Black | | White | Black | | White | Black |
|---|---|---|---|---|---|---|---|---|
| 1 | | | 21 | | | 41 | | |
| 2 | | | 22 | | | 42 | | |
| 3 | | | 23 | | | 43 | | |
| 4 | | | 24 | | | 44 | | |
| 5 | | | 25 | | | 45 | | |
| 6 | | | 26 | | | 46 | | |
| 7 | | | 27 | | | 47 | | |
| 8 | | | 28 | | | 48 | | |
| 9 | | | 29 | | | 49 | | |
| 10 | | | 30 | | | 50 | | |
| 11 | | | 31 | | | 51 | | |
| 12 | | | 32 | | | 52 | | |
| 13 | | | 33 | | | 53 | | |
| 14 | | | 34 | | | 54 | | |
| 15 | | | 35 | | | 55 | | |
| 16 | | | 36 | | | 56 | | |
| 17 | | | 37 | | | 57 | | |
| 18 | | | 38 | | | 58 | | |
| 19 | | | 39 | | | 59 | | |
| 20 | | | 40 | | | 60 | | |

## RESULTS

___ WHITE WON          ___ DRAW          ___ BLACK WON

Notes

| SIGNATURE | SIGNATURE |
|---|---|

# SCORE SHEET

| EVENT | DATE |
|---|---|
| ROUND | BOARD |
| SECTION | OPENING |
| **WHITE (name of player)** | **BLACK (name of player)** |

| | White | Black | | White | Black | | White | Black |
|---|---|---|---|---|---|---|---|---|
| 1 | | | 21 | | | 41 | | |
| 2 | | | 22 | | | 42 | | |
| 3 | | | 23 | | | 43 | | |
| 4 | | | 24 | | | 44 | | |
| 5 | | | 25 | | | 45 | | |
| 6 | | | 26 | | | 46 | | |
| 7 | | | 27 | | | 47 | | |
| 8 | | | 28 | | | 48 | | |
| 9 | | | 29 | | | 49 | | |
| 10 | | | 30 | | | 50 | | |
| 11 | | | 31 | | | 51 | | |
| 12 | | | 32 | | | 52 | | |
| 13 | | | 33 | | | 53 | | |
| 14 | | | 34 | | | 54 | | |
| 15 | | | 35 | | | 55 | | |
| 16 | | | 36 | | | 56 | | |
| 17 | | | 37 | | | 57 | | |
| 18 | | | 38 | | | 58 | | |
| 19 | | | 39 | | | 59 | | |
| 20 | | | 40 | | | 60 | | |

## RESULTS

___ WHITE WON          ___ DRAW          ___ BLACK WON

Notes

SIGNATURE          SIGNATURE

# SCORE SHEET

| EVENT | | DATE | |
|-------|--|------|--|
| ROUND | | BOARD | |
| SECTION | | OPENING | |
| **WHITE (name of player)** | | **BLACK (name of player)** | |

| | White | Black | | White | Black | | White | Black |
|---|-------|-------|---|-------|-------|---|-------|-------|
| 1 | | | 21 | | | 41 | | |
| 2 | | | 22 | | | 42 | | |
| 3 | | | 23 | | | 43 | | |
| 4 | | | 24 | | | 44 | | |
| 5 | | | 25 | | | 45 | | |
| 6 | | | 26 | | | 46 | | |
| 7 | | | 27 | | | 47 | | |
| 8 | | | 28 | | | 48 | | |
| 9 | | | 29 | | | 49 | | |
| 10 | | | 30 | | | 50 | | |
| 11 | | | 31 | | | 51 | | |
| 12 | | | 32 | | | 52 | | |
| 13 | | | 33 | | | 53 | | |
| 14 | | | 34 | | | 54 | | |
| 15 | | | 35 | | | 55 | | |
| 16 | | | 36 | | | 56 | | |
| 17 | | | 37 | | | 57 | | |
| 18 | | | 38 | | | 58 | | |
| 19 | | | 39 | | | 59 | | |
| 20 | | | 40 | | | 60 | | |

## RESULTS

___ WHITE WON          ___ DRAW          ___ BLACK WON

Notes

SIGNATURE                    SIGNATURE

# SCORE SHEET

| EVENT | | DATE | |
|---|---|---|---|
| ROUND | | BOARD | |
| SECTION | | OPENING | |

**WHITE (name of player)**      **BLACK (name of player)**

| | White | Black | | White | Black | | White | Black |
|---|---|---|---|---|---|---|---|---|
| 1 | | | 21 | | | 41 | | |
| 2 | | | 22 | | | 42 | | |
| 3 | | | 23 | | | 43 | | |
| 4 | | | 24 | | | 44 | | |
| 5 | | | 25 | | | 45 | | |
| 6 | | | 26 | | | 46 | | |
| 7 | | | 27 | | | 47 | | |
| 8 | | | 28 | | | 48 | | |
| 9 | | | 29 | | | 49 | | |
| 10 | | | 30 | | | 50 | | |
| 11 | | | 31 | | | 51 | | |
| 12 | | | 32 | | | 52 | | |
| 13 | | | 33 | | | 53 | | |
| 14 | | | 34 | | | 54 | | |
| 15 | | | 35 | | | 55 | | |
| 16 | | | 36 | | | 56 | | |
| 17 | | | 37 | | | 57 | | |
| 18 | | | 38 | | | 58 | | |
| 19 | | | 39 | | | 59 | | |
| 20 | | | 40 | | | 60 | | |

## RESULTS

___ WHITE WON      ___ DRAW      ___ BLACK WON

Notes

8
7
6
5
4
3
2
1
A B C D E F G H

| SIGNATURE | SIGNATURE |
|---|---|

# SCORE SHEET

| EVENT | | DATE | |
|---|---|---|---|
| ROUND | | BOARD | |
| SECTION | | OPENING | |
| **WHITE (name of player)** | | **BLACK (name of player)** | |

| | White | Black | | White | Black | | White | Black |
|---|---|---|---|---|---|---|---|---|
| 1 | | | 21 | | | 41 | | |
| 2 | | | 22 | | | 42 | | |
| 3 | | | 23 | | | 43 | | |
| 4 | | | 24 | | | 44 | | |
| 5 | | | 25 | | | 45 | | |
| 6 | | | 26 | | | 46 | | |
| 7 | | | 27 | | | 47 | | |
| 8 | | | 28 | | | 48 | | |
| 9 | | | 29 | | | 49 | | |
| 10 | | | 30 | | | 50 | | |
| 11 | | | 31 | | | 51 | | |
| 12 | | | 32 | | | 52 | | |
| 13 | | | 33 | | | 53 | | |
| 14 | | | 34 | | | 54 | | |
| 15 | | | 35 | | | 55 | | |
| 16 | | | 36 | | | 56 | | |
| 17 | | | 37 | | | 57 | | |
| 18 | | | 38 | | | 58 | | |
| 19 | | | 39 | | | 59 | | |
| 20 | | | 40 | | | 60 | | |

## RESULTS

___ WHITE WON          ___ DRAW          ___ BLACK WON

Notes

SIGNATURE                    SIGNATURE

# SCORE SHEET

| EVENT | DATE |
|---|---|
| ROUND | BOARD |
| SECTION | OPENING |
| **WHITE (name of player)** | **BLACK (name of player)** |

| | White | Black | | White | Black | | White | Black |
|---|---|---|---|---|---|---|---|---|
| 1 | | | 21 | | | 41 | | |
| 2 | | | 22 | | | 42 | | |
| 3 | | | 23 | | | 43 | | |
| 4 | | | 24 | | | 44 | | |
| 5 | | | 25 | | | 45 | | |
| 6 | | | 26 | | | 46 | | |
| 7 | | | 27 | | | 47 | | |
| 8 | | | 28 | | | 48 | | |
| 9 | | | 29 | | | 49 | | |
| 10 | | | 30 | | | 50 | | |
| 11 | | | 31 | | | 51 | | |
| 12 | | | 32 | | | 52 | | |
| 13 | | | 33 | | | 53 | | |
| 14 | | | 34 | | | 54 | | |
| 15 | | | 35 | | | 55 | | |
| 16 | | | 36 | | | 56 | | |
| 17 | | | 37 | | | 57 | | |
| 18 | | | 38 | | | 58 | | |
| 19 | | | 39 | | | 59 | | |
| 20 | | | 40 | | | 60 | | |

## RESULTS

___ WHITE WON          ___ DRAW          ___ BLACK WON

Notes

8
7
6
5
4
3
2
1
A B C D E F G H

| SIGNATURE | SIGNATURE |
|---|---|

# SCORE SHEET

| EVENT | | DATE | |
|---|---|---|---|
| ROUND | | BOARD | |
| SECTION | | OPENING | |
| **WHITE (name of player)** | | **BLACK (name of player)** | |

| | White | Black | | White | Black | | White | Black |
|---|---|---|---|---|---|---|---|---|
| 1 | | | 21 | | | 41 | | |
| 2 | | | 22 | | | 42 | | |
| 3 | | | 23 | | | 43 | | |
| 4 | | | 24 | | | 44 | | |
| 5 | | | 25 | | | 45 | | |
| 6 | | | 26 | | | 46 | | |
| 7 | | | 27 | | | 47 | | |
| 8 | | | 28 | | | 48 | | |
| 9 | | | 29 | | | 49 | | |
| 10 | | | 30 | | | 50 | | |
| 11 | | | 31 | | | 51 | | |
| 12 | | | 32 | | | 52 | | |
| 13 | | | 33 | | | 53 | | |
| 14 | | | 34 | | | 54 | | |
| 15 | | | 35 | | | 55 | | |
| 16 | | | 36 | | | 56 | | |
| 17 | | | 37 | | | 57 | | |
| 18 | | | 38 | | | 58 | | |
| 19 | | | 39 | | | 59 | | |
| 20 | | | 40 | | | 60 | | |

## RESULTS

___ WHITE WON        ___ DRAW        ___ BLACK WON

Notes

| SIGNATURE | | SIGNATURE | |

# SCORE SHEET

| EVENT | DATE |
|---|---|
| ROUND | BOARD |
| SECTION | OPENING |
| **WHITE (name of player)** | **BLACK (name of player)** |

| | White | Black | | White | Black | | White | Black |
|---|---|---|---|---|---|---|---|---|
| 1 | | | 21 | | | 41 | | |
| 2 | | | 22 | | | 42 | | |
| 3 | | | 23 | | | 43 | | |
| 4 | | | 24 | | | 44 | | |
| 5 | | | 25 | | | 45 | | |
| 6 | | | 26 | | | 46 | | |
| 7 | | | 27 | | | 47 | | |
| 8 | | | 28 | | | 48 | | |
| 9 | | | 29 | | | 49 | | |
| 10 | | | 30 | | | 50 | | |
| 11 | | | 31 | | | 51 | | |
| 12 | | | 32 | | | 52 | | |
| 13 | | | 33 | | | 53 | | |
| 14 | | | 34 | | | 54 | | |
| 15 | | | 35 | | | 55 | | |
| 16 | | | 36 | | | 56 | | |
| 17 | | | 37 | | | 57 | | |
| 18 | | | 38 | | | 58 | | |
| 19 | | | 39 | | | 59 | | |
| 20 | | | 40 | | | 60 | | |

## RESULTS

___ WHITE WON          ___ DRAW          ___ BLACK WON

Notes

```
8
7
6
5
4
3
2
1
  A B C D E F G H
```

| SIGNATURE | SIGNATURE |
|---|---|

# SCORE SHEET

| EVENT | | DATE | |
|---|---|---|---|
| ROUND | | BOARD | |
| SECTION | | OPENING | |
| **WHITE (name of player)** | | **BLACK (name of player)** | |

| | White | Black | | White | Black | | White | Black |
|---|---|---|---|---|---|---|---|---|
| 1 | | | 21 | | | 41 | | |
| 2 | | | 22 | | | 42 | | |
| 3 | | | 23 | | | 43 | | |
| 4 | | | 24 | | | 44 | | |
| 5 | | | 25 | | | 45 | | |
| 6 | | | 26 | | | 46 | | |
| 7 | | | 27 | | | 47 | | |
| 8 | | | 28 | | | 48 | | |
| 9 | | | 29 | | | 49 | | |
| 10 | | | 30 | | | 50 | | |
| 11 | | | 31 | | | 51 | | |
| 12 | | | 32 | | | 52 | | |
| 13 | | | 33 | | | 53 | | |
| 14 | | | 34 | | | 54 | | |
| 15 | | | 35 | | | 55 | | |
| 16 | | | 36 | | | 56 | | |
| 17 | | | 37 | | | 57 | | |
| 18 | | | 38 | | | 58 | | |
| 19 | | | 39 | | | 59 | | |
| 20 | | | 40 | | | 60 | | |

## RESULTS

___ WHITE WON          ___ DRAW          ___ BLACK WON

Notes

| SIGNATURE | SIGNATURE |
|---|---|

# SCORE SHEET

| EVENT | DATE |
|---|---|
| ROUND | BOARD |
| SECTION | OPENING |
| WHITE (name of player) | BLACK (name of player) |

| | White | Black | | White | Black | | White | Black |
|---|---|---|---|---|---|---|---|---|
| 1 | | | 21 | | | 41 | | |
| 2 | | | 22 | | | 42 | | |
| 3 | | | 23 | | | 43 | | |
| 4 | | | 24 | | | 44 | | |
| 5 | | | 25 | | | 45 | | |
| 6 | | | 26 | | | 46 | | |
| 7 | | | 27 | | | 47 | | |
| 8 | | | 28 | | | 48 | | |
| 9 | | | 29 | | | 49 | | |
| 10 | | | 30 | | | 50 | | |
| 11 | | | 31 | | | 51 | | |
| 12 | | | 32 | | | 52 | | |
| 13 | | | 33 | | | 53 | | |
| 14 | | | 34 | | | 54 | | |
| 15 | | | 35 | | | 55 | | |
| 16 | | | 36 | | | 56 | | |
| 17 | | | 37 | | | 57 | | |
| 18 | | | 38 | | | 58 | | |
| 19 | | | 39 | | | 59 | | |
| 20 | | | 40 | | | 60 | | |

## RESULTS

___ WHITE WON          ___ DRAW          ___ BLACK WON

Notes

| SIGNATURE | SIGNATURE |
|---|---|

# SCORE SHEET

| EVENT | | DATE | |
|---|---|---|---|
| ROUND | | BOARD | |
| SECTION | | OPENING | |
| **WHITE (name of player)** | | **BLACK (name of player)** | |

| | White | Black | | White | Black | | White | Black |
|---|---|---|---|---|---|---|---|---|
| 1 | | | 21 | | | 41 | | |
| 2 | | | 22 | | | 42 | | |
| 3 | | | 23 | | | 43 | | |
| 4 | | | 24 | | | 44 | | |
| 5 | | | 25 | | | 45 | | |
| 6 | | | 26 | | | 46 | | |
| 7 | | | 27 | | | 47 | | |
| 8 | | | 28 | | | 48 | | |
| 9 | | | 29 | | | 49 | | |
| 10 | | | 30 | | | 50 | | |
| 11 | | | 31 | | | 51 | | |
| 12 | | | 32 | | | 52 | | |
| 13 | | | 33 | | | 53 | | |
| 14 | | | 34 | | | 54 | | |
| 15 | | | 35 | | | 55 | | |
| 16 | | | 36 | | | 56 | | |
| 17 | | | 37 | | | 57 | | |
| 18 | | | 38 | | | 58 | | |
| 19 | | | 39 | | | 59 | | |
| 20 | | | 40 | | | 60 | | |

## RESULTS

___ WHITE WON        ___ DRAW        ___ BLACK WON

Notes

| SIGNATURE | | SIGNATURE | |
|---|---|---|---|

# SCORE SHEET

| EVENT | | | | | DATE | | | |
|---|---|---|---|---|---|---|---|---|
| ROUND | | | | | BOARD | | | |
| SECTION | | | | | OPENING | | | |

**WHITE (name of player)**        **BLACK (name of player)**

| | White | Black | | White | Black | | White | Black |
|---|---|---|---|---|---|---|---|---|
| 1 | | | 21 | | | 41 | | |
| 2 | | | 22 | | | 42 | | |
| 3 | | | 23 | | | 43 | | |
| 4 | | | 24 | | | 44 | | |
| 5 | | | 25 | | | 45 | | |
| 6 | | | 26 | | | 46 | | |
| 7 | | | 27 | | | 47 | | |
| 8 | | | 28 | | | 48 | | |
| 9 | | | 29 | | | 49 | | |
| 10 | | | 30 | | | 50 | | |
| 11 | | | 31 | | | 51 | | |
| 12 | | | 32 | | | 52 | | |
| 13 | | | 33 | | | 53 | | |
| 14 | | | 34 | | | 54 | | |
| 15 | | | 35 | | | 55 | | |
| 16 | | | 36 | | | 56 | | |
| 17 | | | 37 | | | 57 | | |
| 18 | | | 38 | | | 58 | | |
| 19 | | | 39 | | | 59 | | |
| 20 | | | 40 | | | 60 | | |

## RESULTS

___ WHITE WON        ___ DRAW        ___ BLACK WON

Notes

| SIGNATURE | SIGNATURE |
|---|---|

# SCORE SHEET

| EVENT | DATE |
|---|---|
| ROUND | BOARD |
| SECTION | OPENING |
| **WHITE (name of player)** | **BLACK (name of player)** |

| | White | Black | | White | Black | | White | Black |
|---|---|---|---|---|---|---|---|---|
| 1 | | | 21 | | | 41 | | |
| 2 | | | 22 | | | 42 | | |
| 3 | | | 23 | | | 43 | | |
| 4 | | | 24 | | | 44 | | |
| 5 | | | 25 | | | 45 | | |
| 6 | | | 26 | | | 46 | | |
| 7 | | | 27 | | | 47 | | |
| 8 | | | 28 | | | 48 | | |
| 9 | | | 29 | | | 49 | | |
| 10 | | | 30 | | | 50 | | |
| 11 | | | 31 | | | 51 | | |
| 12 | | | 32 | | | 52 | | |
| 13 | | | 33 | | | 53 | | |
| 14 | | | 34 | | | 54 | | |
| 15 | | | 35 | | | 55 | | |
| 16 | | | 36 | | | 56 | | |
| 17 | | | 37 | | | 57 | | |
| 18 | | | 38 | | | 58 | | |
| 19 | | | 39 | | | 59 | | |
| 20 | | | 40 | | | 60 | | |

## RESULTS

___ WHITE WON          ___ DRAW          ___ BLACK WON

Notes

SIGNATURE          SIGNATURE

# SCORE SHEET

| EVENT | DATE |
|---|---|
| ROUND | BOARD |
| SECTION | OPENING |
| **WHITE (name of player)** | **BLACK (name of player)** |

| | White | Black | | White | Black | | White | Black |
|---|---|---|---|---|---|---|---|---|
| 1 | | | 21 | | | 41 | | |
| 2 | | | 22 | | | 42 | | |
| 3 | | | 23 | | | 43 | | |
| 4 | | | 24 | | | 44 | | |
| 5 | | | 25 | | | 45 | | |
| 6 | | | 26 | | | 46 | | |
| 7 | | | 27 | | | 47 | | |
| 8 | | | 28 | | | 48 | | |
| 9 | | | 29 | | | 49 | | |
| 10 | | | 30 | | | 50 | | |
| 11 | | | 31 | | | 51 | | |
| 12 | | | 32 | | | 52 | | |
| 13 | | | 33 | | | 53 | | |
| 14 | | | 34 | | | 54 | | |
| 15 | | | 35 | | | 55 | | |
| 16 | | | 36 | | | 56 | | |
| 17 | | | 37 | | | 57 | | |
| 18 | | | 38 | | | 58 | | |
| 19 | | | 39 | | | 59 | | |
| 20 | | | 40 | | | 60 | | |

## RESULTS

___ WHITE WON          ___ DRAW          ___ BLACK WON

Notes

8
7
6
5
4
3
2
1
A B C D E F G H

| SIGNATURE | SIGNATURE |
|---|---|

# SCORE SHEET

| EVENT | | DATE |
|---|---|---|
| ROUND | | BOARD |
| SECTION | | OPENING |
| **WHITE (name of player)** | | **BLACK (name of player)** |

| | White | Black | | White | Black | | White | Black |
|---|---|---|---|---|---|---|---|---|
| 1 | | | 21 | | | 41 | | |
| 2 | | | 22 | | | 42 | | |
| 3 | | | 23 | | | 43 | | |
| 4 | | | 24 | | | 44 | | |
| 5 | | | 25 | | | 45 | | |
| 6 | | | 26 | | | 46 | | |
| 7 | | | 27 | | | 47 | | |
| 8 | | | 28 | | | 48 | | |
| 9 | | | 29 | | | 49 | | |
| 10 | | | 30 | | | 50 | | |
| 11 | | | 31 | | | 51 | | |
| 12 | | | 32 | | | 52 | | |
| 13 | | | 33 | | | 53 | | |
| 14 | | | 34 | | | 54 | | |
| 15 | | | 35 | | | 55 | | |
| 16 | | | 36 | | | 56 | | |
| 17 | | | 37 | | | 57 | | |
| 18 | | | 38 | | | 58 | | |
| 19 | | | 39 | | | 59 | | |
| 20 | | | 40 | | | 60 | | |

## RESULTS

___ WHITE WON          ___ DRAW          ___ BLACK WON

Notes

SIGNATURE          SIGNATURE

# SCORE SHEET

| EVENT | DATE |
|---|---|
| ROUND | BOARD |
| SECTION | OPENING |
| **WHITE (name of player)** | **BLACK (name of player)** |

| | White | Black | | White | Black | | White | Black |
|---|---|---|---|---|---|---|---|---|
| 1 | | | 21 | | | 41 | | |
| 2 | | | 22 | | | 42 | | |
| 3 | | | 23 | | | 43 | | |
| 4 | | | 24 | | | 44 | | |
| 5 | | | 25 | | | 45 | | |
| 6 | | | 26 | | | 46 | | |
| 7 | | | 27 | | | 47 | | |
| 8 | | | 28 | | | 48 | | |
| 9 | | | 29 | | | 49 | | |
| 10 | | | 30 | | | 50 | | |
| 11 | | | 31 | | | 51 | | |
| 12 | | | 32 | | | 52 | | |
| 13 | | | 33 | | | 53 | | |
| 14 | | | 34 | | | 54 | | |
| 15 | | | 35 | | | 55 | | |
| 16 | | | 36 | | | 56 | | |
| 17 | | | 37 | | | 57 | | |
| 18 | | | 38 | | | 58 | | |
| 19 | | | 39 | | | 59 | | |
| 20 | | | 40 | | | 60 | | |

## RESULTS

___ WHITE WON          ___ DRAW          ___ BLACK WON

Notes

| SIGNATURE | SIGNATURE |
|---|---|

# SCORE SHEET

| | | | | | |
|---|---|---|---|---|---|
| EVENT | | | DATE | | |
| ROUND | | | BOARD | | |
| SECTION | | | OPENING | | |
| **WHITE (name of player)** | | | **BLACK (name of player)** | | |

| | White | Black | | White | Black | | White | Black |
|---|---|---|---|---|---|---|---|---|
| 1 | | | 21 | | | 41 | | |
| 2 | | | 22 | | | 42 | | |
| 3 | | | 23 | | | 43 | | |
| 4 | | | 24 | | | 44 | | |
| 5 | | | 25 | | | 45 | | |
| 6 | | | 26 | | | 46 | | |
| 7 | | | 27 | | | 47 | | |
| 8 | | | 28 | | | 48 | | |
| 9 | | | 29 | | | 49 | | |
| 10 | | | 30 | | | 50 | | |
| 11 | | | 31 | | | 51 | | |
| 12 | | | 32 | | | 52 | | |
| 13 | | | 33 | | | 53 | | |
| 14 | | | 34 | | | 54 | | |
| 15 | | | 35 | | | 55 | | |
| 16 | | | 36 | | | 56 | | |
| 17 | | | 37 | | | 57 | | |
| 18 | | | 38 | | | 58 | | |
| 19 | | | 39 | | | 59 | | |
| 20 | | | 40 | | | 60 | | |

## RESULTS

___ WHITE WON          ___ DRAW          ___ BLACK WON

Notes

SIGNATURE                    SIGNATURE

# SCORE SHEET

| EVENT | DATE |
|---|---|
| ROUND | BOARD |
| SECTION | OPENING |
| **WHITE (name of player)** | **BLACK (name of player)** |

| | White | Black | | White | Black | | White | Black |
|---|---|---|---|---|---|---|---|---|
| 1 | | | 21 | | | 41 | | |
| 2 | | | 22 | | | 42 | | |
| 3 | | | 23 | | | 43 | | |
| 4 | | | 24 | | | 44 | | |
| 5 | | | 25 | | | 45 | | |
| 6 | | | 26 | | | 46 | | |
| 7 | | | 27 | | | 47 | | |
| 8 | | | 28 | | | 48 | | |
| 9 | | | 29 | | | 49 | | |
| 10 | | | 30 | | | 50 | | |
| 11 | | | 31 | | | 51 | | |
| 12 | | | 32 | | | 52 | | |
| 13 | | | 33 | | | 53 | | |
| 14 | | | 34 | | | 54 | | |
| 15 | | | 35 | | | 55 | | |
| 16 | | | 36 | | | 56 | | |
| 17 | | | 37 | | | 57 | | |
| 18 | | | 38 | | | 58 | | |
| 19 | | | 39 | | | 59 | | |
| 20 | | | 40 | | | 60 | | |

## RESULTS

___ WHITE WON        ___ DRAW        ___ BLACK WON

Notes

8
7
6
5
4
3
2
1
A B C D E F G H

| SIGNATURE | SIGNATURE |
|---|---|

# SCORE SHEET

| EVENT | | DATE | |
| ROUND | | BOARD | |
| SECTION | | OPENING | |
| **WHITE (name of player)** | | **BLACK (name of player)** | |

| | White | Black | | White | Black | | White | Black |
|---|---|---|---|---|---|---|---|---|
| 1 | | | 21 | | | 41 | | |
| 2 | | | 22 | | | 42 | | |
| 3 | | | 23 | | | 43 | | |
| 4 | | | 24 | | | 44 | | |
| 5 | | | 25 | | | 45 | | |
| 6 | | | 26 | | | 46 | | |
| 7 | | | 27 | | | 47 | | |
| 8 | | | 28 | | | 48 | | |
| 9 | | | 29 | | | 49 | | |
| 10 | | | 30 | | | 50 | | |
| 11 | | | 31 | | | 51 | | |
| 12 | | | 32 | | | 52 | | |
| 13 | | | 33 | | | 53 | | |
| 14 | | | 34 | | | 54 | | |
| 15 | | | 35 | | | 55 | | |
| 16 | | | 36 | | | 56 | | |
| 17 | | | 37 | | | 57 | | |
| 18 | | | 38 | | | 58 | | |
| 19 | | | 39 | | | 59 | | |
| 20 | | | 40 | | | 60 | | |

## RESULTS

___ WHITE WON          ___ DRAW          ___ BLACK WON

Notes

| | | | | | | | |
|---|---|---|---|---|---|---|---|
| 8 | | | | | | | |
| 7 | | | | | | | |
| 6 | | | | | | | |
| 5 | | | | | | | |
| 4 | | | | | | | |
| 3 | | | | | | | |
| 2 | | | | | | | |
| 1 | | | | | | | |

A B C D E F G H

SIGNATURE          SIGNATURE

# SCORE SHEET

| EVENT | | DATE | |
|---|---|---|---|
| ROUND | | BOARD | |
| SECTION | | OPENING | |
| **WHITE (name of player)** | | **BLACK (name of player)** | |

| | White | Black | | White | Black | | White | Black |
|---|---|---|---|---|---|---|---|---|
| 1 | | | 21 | | | 41 | | |
| 2 | | | 22 | | | 42 | | |
| 3 | | | 23 | | | 43 | | |
| 4 | | | 24 | | | 44 | | |
| 5 | | | 25 | | | 45 | | |
| 6 | | | 26 | | | 46 | | |
| 7 | | | 27 | | | 47 | | |
| 8 | | | 28 | | | 48 | | |
| 9 | | | 29 | | | 49 | | |
| 10 | | | 30 | | | 50 | | |
| 11 | | | 31 | | | 51 | | |
| 12 | | | 32 | | | 52 | | |
| 13 | | | 33 | | | 53 | | |
| 14 | | | 34 | | | 54 | | |
| 15 | | | 35 | | | 55 | | |
| 16 | | | 36 | | | 56 | | |
| 17 | | | 37 | | | 57 | | |
| 18 | | | 38 | | | 58 | | |
| 19 | | | 39 | | | 59 | | |
| 20 | | | 40 | | | 60 | | |

## RESULTS

___ WHITE WON        ___ DRAW        ___ BLACK WON

Notes

| SIGNATURE | | SIGNATURE | |

# SCORE SHEET

| EVENT | | DATE | |
|---|---|---|---|
| ROUND | | BOARD | |
| SECTION | | OPENING | |

**WHITE (name of player)** | | **BLACK (name of player)** |

| | White | Black | | White | Black | | White | Black |
|---|---|---|---|---|---|---|---|---|
| 1 | | | 21 | | | 41 | | |
| 2 | | | 22 | | | 42 | | |
| 3 | | | 23 | | | 43 | | |
| 4 | | | 24 | | | 44 | | |
| 5 | | | 25 | | | 45 | | |
| 6 | | | 26 | | | 46 | | |
| 7 | | | 27 | | | 47 | | |
| 8 | | | 28 | | | 48 | | |
| 9 | | | 29 | | | 49 | | |
| 10 | | | 30 | | | 50 | | |
| 11 | | | 31 | | | 51 | | |
| 12 | | | 32 | | | 52 | | |
| 13 | | | 33 | | | 53 | | |
| 14 | | | 34 | | | 54 | | |
| 15 | | | 35 | | | 55 | | |
| 16 | | | 36 | | | 56 | | |
| 17 | | | 37 | | | 57 | | |
| 18 | | | 38 | | | 58 | | |
| 19 | | | 39 | | | 59 | | |
| 20 | | | 40 | | | 60 | | |

## RESULTS

___ WHITE WON          ___ DRAW          ___ BLACK WON

Notes

SIGNATURE | SIGNATURE

# SCORE SHEET

| EVENT | DATE |
|---|---|
| ROUND | BOARD |
| SECTION | OPENING |
| **WHITE (name of player)** | **BLACK (name of player)** |

| | White | Black | | White | Black | | White | Black |
|---|---|---|---|---|---|---|---|---|
| 1 | | | 21 | | | 41 | | |
| 2 | | | 22 | | | 42 | | |
| 3 | | | 23 | | | 43 | | |
| 4 | | | 24 | | | 44 | | |
| 5 | | | 25 | | | 45 | | |
| 6 | | | 26 | | | 46 | | |
| 7 | | | 27 | | | 47 | | |
| 8 | | | 28 | | | 48 | | |
| 9 | | | 29 | | | 49 | | |
| 10 | | | 30 | | | 50 | | |
| 11 | | | 31 | | | 51 | | |
| 12 | | | 32 | | | 52 | | |
| 13 | | | 33 | | | 53 | | |
| 14 | | | 34 | | | 54 | | |
| 15 | | | 35 | | | 55 | | |
| 16 | | | 36 | | | 56 | | |
| 17 | | | 37 | | | 57 | | |
| 18 | | | 38 | | | 58 | | |
| 19 | | | 39 | | | 59 | | |
| 20 | | | 40 | | | 60 | | |

## RESULTS

___ WHITE WON        ___ DRAW        ___ BLACK WON

Notes

8 7 6 5 4 3 2 1
A B C D E F G H

| SIGNATURE | SIGNATURE |
|---|---|

# SCORE SHEET

| EVENT | | DATE | |
|---|---|---|---|
| ROUND | | BOARD | |
| SECTION | | OPENING | |
| **WHITE (name of player)** | | **BLACK (name of player)** | |

| | White | Black | | White | Black | | White | Black |
|---|---|---|---|---|---|---|---|---|
| 1 | | | 21 | | | 41 | | |
| 2 | | | 22 | | | 42 | | |
| 3 | | | 23 | | | 43 | | |
| 4 | | | 24 | | | 44 | | |
| 5 | | | 25 | | | 45 | | |
| 6 | | | 26 | | | 46 | | |
| 7 | | | 27 | | | 47 | | |
| 8 | | | 28 | | | 48 | | |
| 9 | | | 29 | | | 49 | | |
| 10 | | | 30 | | | 50 | | |
| 11 | | | 31 | | | 51 | | |
| 12 | | | 32 | | | 52 | | |
| 13 | | | 33 | | | 53 | | |
| 14 | | | 34 | | | 54 | | |
| 15 | | | 35 | | | 55 | | |
| 16 | | | 36 | | | 56 | | |
| 17 | | | 37 | | | 57 | | |
| 18 | | | 38 | | | 58 | | |
| 19 | | | 39 | | | 59 | | |
| 20 | | | 40 | | | 60 | | |

## RESULTS

___ WHITE WON          ___ DRAW          ___ BLACK WON

Notes

SIGNATURE                              SIGNATURE

# SCORE SHEET

| EVENT | | DATE | |
| --- | --- | --- | --- |
| ROUND | | BOARD | |
| SECTION | | OPENING | |
| **WHITE (name of player)** | | **BLACK (name of player)** | |

| | White | Black | | White | Black | | White | Black |
| --- | --- | --- | --- | --- | --- | --- | --- | --- |
| 1 | | | 21 | | | 41 | | |
| 2 | | | 22 | | | 42 | | |
| 3 | | | 23 | | | 43 | | |
| 4 | | | 24 | | | 44 | | |
| 5 | | | 25 | | | 45 | | |
| 6 | | | 26 | | | 46 | | |
| 7 | | | 27 | | | 47 | | |
| 8 | | | 28 | | | 48 | | |
| 9 | | | 29 | | | 49 | | |
| 10 | | | 30 | | | 50 | | |
| 11 | | | 31 | | | 51 | | |
| 12 | | | 32 | | | 52 | | |
| 13 | | | 33 | | | 53 | | |
| 14 | | | 34 | | | 54 | | |
| 15 | | | 35 | | | 55 | | |
| 16 | | | 36 | | | 56 | | |
| 17 | | | 37 | | | 57 | | |
| 18 | | | 38 | | | 58 | | |
| 19 | | | 39 | | | 59 | | |
| 20 | | | 40 | | | 60 | | |

## RESULTS

___ WHITE WON          ___ DRAW          ___ BLACK WON

Notes

| SIGNATURE | | SIGNATURE | |

# SCORE SHEET

| EVENT | | DATE | |
|---|---|---|---|
| ROUND | | BOARD | |
| SECTION | | OPENING | |
| **WHITE (name of player)** | | **BLACK (name of player)** | |

| | White | Black | | White | Black | | White | Black |
|---|---|---|---|---|---|---|---|---|
| 1 | | | 21 | | | 41 | | |
| 2 | | | 22 | | | 42 | | |
| 3 | | | 23 | | | 43 | | |
| 4 | | | 24 | | | 44 | | |
| 5 | | | 25 | | | 45 | | |
| 6 | | | 26 | | | 46 | | |
| 7 | | | 27 | | | 47 | | |
| 8 | | | 28 | | | 48 | | |
| 9 | | | 29 | | | 49 | | |
| 10 | | | 30 | | | 50 | | |
| 11 | | | 31 | | | 51 | | |
| 12 | | | 32 | | | 52 | | |
| 13 | | | 33 | | | 53 | | |
| 14 | | | 34 | | | 54 | | |
| 15 | | | 35 | | | 55 | | |
| 16 | | | 36 | | | 56 | | |
| 17 | | | 37 | | | 57 | | |
| 18 | | | 38 | | | 58 | | |
| 19 | | | 39 | | | 59 | | |
| 20 | | | 40 | | | 60 | | |

## RESULTS

___ WHITE WON       ___ DRAW       ___ BLACK WON

Notes

| SIGNATURE | SIGNATURE |
|---|---|

# SCORE SHEET

| EVENT | DATE |
|---|---|
| ROUND | BOARD |
| SECTION | OPENING |
| **WHITE (name of player)** | **BLACK (name of player)** |

| | White | Black | | White | Black | | White | Black |
|---|---|---|---|---|---|---|---|---|
| 1 | | | 21 | | | 41 | | |
| 2 | | | 22 | | | 42 | | |
| 3 | | | 23 | | | 43 | | |
| 4 | | | 24 | | | 44 | | |
| 5 | | | 25 | | | 45 | | |
| 6 | | | 26 | | | 46 | | |
| 7 | | | 27 | | | 47 | | |
| 8 | | | 28 | | | 48 | | |
| 9 | | | 29 | | | 49 | | |
| 10 | | | 30 | | | 50 | | |
| 11 | | | 31 | | | 51 | | |
| 12 | | | 32 | | | 52 | | |
| 13 | | | 33 | | | 53 | | |
| 14 | | | 34 | | | 54 | | |
| 15 | | | 35 | | | 55 | | |
| 16 | | | 36 | | | 56 | | |
| 17 | | | 37 | | | 57 | | |
| 18 | | | 38 | | | 58 | | |
| 19 | | | 39 | | | 59 | | |
| 20 | | | 40 | | | 60 | | |

## RESULTS

___ WHITE WON          ___ DRAW          ___ BLACK WON

Notes

SIGNATURE                    SIGNATURE

# SCORE SHEET

| EVENT | DATE |
|---|---|
| ROUND | BOARD |
| SECTION | OPENING |
| **WHITE (name of player)** | **BLACK (name of player)** |

| | White | Black | | White | Black | | White | Black |
|---|---|---|---|---|---|---|---|---|
| 1 | | | 21 | | | 41 | | |
| 2 | | | 22 | | | 42 | | |
| 3 | | | 23 | | | 43 | | |
| 4 | | | 24 | | | 44 | | |
| 5 | | | 25 | | | 45 | | |
| 6 | | | 26 | | | 46 | | |
| 7 | | | 27 | | | 47 | | |
| 8 | | | 28 | | | 48 | | |
| 9 | | | 29 | | | 49 | | |
| 10 | | | 30 | | | 50 | | |
| 11 | | | 31 | | | 51 | | |
| 12 | | | 32 | | | 52 | | |
| 13 | | | 33 | | | 53 | | |
| 14 | | | 34 | | | 54 | | |
| 15 | | | 35 | | | 55 | | |
| 16 | | | 36 | | | 56 | | |
| 17 | | | 37 | | | 57 | | |
| 18 | | | 38 | | | 58 | | |
| 19 | | | 39 | | | 59 | | |
| 20 | | | 40 | | | 60 | | |

## RESULTS

___ WHITE WON           ___ DRAW           ___ BLACK WON

Notes

| SIGNATURE | SIGNATURE |
|---|---|

# SCORE SHEET

| EVENT | | DATE | |
|---|---|---|---|
| ROUND | | BOARD | |
| SECTION | | OPENING | |

**WHITE (name of player)**      **BLACK (name of player)**

| | White | Black | | White | Black | | White | Black |
|---|---|---|---|---|---|---|---|---|
| 1 | | | 21 | | | 41 | | |
| 2 | | | 22 | | | 42 | | |
| 3 | | | 23 | | | 43 | | |
| 4 | | | 24 | | | 44 | | |
| 5 | | | 25 | | | 45 | | |
| 6 | | | 26 | | | 46 | | |
| 7 | | | 27 | | | 47 | | |
| 8 | | | 28 | | | 48 | | |
| 9 | | | 29 | | | 49 | | |
| 10 | | | 30 | | | 50 | | |
| 11 | | | 31 | | | 51 | | |
| 12 | | | 32 | | | 52 | | |
| 13 | | | 33 | | | 53 | | |
| 14 | | | 34 | | | 54 | | |
| 15 | | | 35 | | | 55 | | |
| 16 | | | 36 | | | 56 | | |
| 17 | | | 37 | | | 57 | | |
| 18 | | | 38 | | | 58 | | |
| 19 | | | 39 | | | 59 | | |
| 20 | | | 40 | | | 60 | | |

## RESULTS

___ WHITE WON      ___ DRAW      ___ BLACK WON

Notes

```
8
7
6
5
4
3
2
1
  A B C D E F G H
```

| SIGNATURE | | SIGNATURE | |
|---|---|---|---|

# SCORE SHEET

| EVENT | | DATE | |
|---|---|---|---|
| ROUND | | BOARD | |
| SECTION | | OPENING | |
| **WHITE (name of player)** | | **BLACK (name of player)** | |

| | White | Black | | White | Black | | White | Black |
|---|---|---|---|---|---|---|---|---|
| 1 | | | 21 | | | 41 | | |
| 2 | | | 22 | | | 42 | | |
| 3 | | | 23 | | | 43 | | |
| 4 | | | 24 | | | 44 | | |
| 5 | | | 25 | | | 45 | | |
| 6 | | | 26 | | | 46 | | |
| 7 | | | 27 | | | 47 | | |
| 8 | | | 28 | | | 48 | | |
| 9 | | | 29 | | | 49 | | |
| 10 | | | 30 | | | 50 | | |
| 11 | | | 31 | | | 51 | | |
| 12 | | | 32 | | | 52 | | |
| 13 | | | 33 | | | 53 | | |
| 14 | | | 34 | | | 54 | | |
| 15 | | | 35 | | | 55 | | |
| 16 | | | 36 | | | 56 | | |
| 17 | | | 37 | | | 57 | | |
| 18 | | | 38 | | | 58 | | |
| 19 | | | 39 | | | 59 | | |
| 20 | | | 40 | | | 60 | | |

## RESULTS

___ WHITE WON          ___ DRAW          ___ BLACK WON

Notes

SIGNATURE                    SIGNATURE

# SCORE SHEET

| EVENT | | DATE | |
|---|---|---|---|
| ROUND | | BOARD | |
| SECTION | | OPENING | |
| **WHITE (name of player)** | | **BLACK (name of player)** | |

| | White | Black | | White | Black | | White | Black |
|---|---|---|---|---|---|---|---|---|
| 1 | | | 21 | | | 41 | | |
| 2 | | | 22 | | | 42 | | |
| 3 | | | 23 | | | 43 | | |
| 4 | | | 24 | | | 44 | | |
| 5 | | | 25 | | | 45 | | |
| 6 | | | 26 | | | 46 | | |
| 7 | | | 27 | | | 47 | | |
| 8 | | | 28 | | | 48 | | |
| 9 | | | 29 | | | 49 | | |
| 10 | | | 30 | | | 50 | | |
| 11 | | | 31 | | | 51 | | |
| 12 | | | 32 | | | 52 | | |
| 13 | | | 33 | | | 53 | | |
| 14 | | | 34 | | | 54 | | |
| 15 | | | 35 | | | 55 | | |
| 16 | | | 36 | | | 56 | | |
| 17 | | | 37 | | | 57 | | |
| 18 | | | 38 | | | 58 | | |
| 19 | | | 39 | | | 59 | | |
| 20 | | | 40 | | | 60 | | |

## RESULTS

___ WHITE WON        ___ DRAW        ___ BLACK WON

Notes

8
7
6
5
4
3
2
1
A B C D E F G H

| SIGNATURE | | SIGNATURE | |

# SCORE SHEET

| EVENT | | DATE | |
|---|---|---|---|
| ROUND | | BOARD | |
| SECTION | | OPENING | |
| **WHITE (name of player)** | | **BLACK (name of player)** | |

| | White | Black | | White | Black | | White | Black |
|---|---|---|---|---|---|---|---|---|
| 1 | | | 21 | | | 41 | | |
| 2 | | | 22 | | | 42 | | |
| 3 | | | 23 | | | 43 | | |
| 4 | | | 24 | | | 44 | | |
| 5 | | | 25 | | | 45 | | |
| 6 | | | 26 | | | 46 | | |
| 7 | | | 27 | | | 47 | | |
| 8 | | | 28 | | | 48 | | |
| 9 | | | 29 | | | 49 | | |
| 10 | | | 30 | | | 50 | | |
| 11 | | | 31 | | | 51 | | |
| 12 | | | 32 | | | 52 | | |
| 13 | | | 33 | | | 53 | | |
| 14 | | | 34 | | | 54 | | |
| 15 | | | 35 | | | 55 | | |
| 16 | | | 36 | | | 56 | | |
| 17 | | | 37 | | | 57 | | |
| 18 | | | 38 | | | 58 | | |
| 19 | | | 39 | | | 59 | | |
| 20 | | | 40 | | | 60 | | |

## RESULTS

___ WHITE WON          ___ DRAW          ___ BLACK WON

Notes

SIGNATURE                    SIGNATURE

# SCORE SHEET

| EVENT | DATE |
|---|---|
| ROUND | BOARD |
| SECTION | OPENING |
| **WHITE (name of player)** | **BLACK (name of player)** |

| | White | Black | | White | Black | | White | Black |
|---|---|---|---|---|---|---|---|---|
| 1 | | | 21 | | | 41 | | |
| 2 | | | 22 | | | 42 | | |
| 3 | | | 23 | | | 43 | | |
| 4 | | | 24 | | | 44 | | |
| 5 | | | 25 | | | 45 | | |
| 6 | | | 26 | | | 46 | | |
| 7 | | | 27 | | | 47 | | |
| 8 | | | 28 | | | 48 | | |
| 9 | | | 29 | | | 49 | | |
| 10 | | | 30 | | | 50 | | |
| 11 | | | 31 | | | 51 | | |
| 12 | | | 32 | | | 52 | | |
| 13 | | | 33 | | | 53 | | |
| 14 | | | 34 | | | 54 | | |
| 15 | | | 35 | | | 55 | | |
| 16 | | | 36 | | | 56 | | |
| 17 | | | 37 | | | 57 | | |
| 18 | | | 38 | | | 58 | | |
| 19 | | | 39 | | | 59 | | |
| 20 | | | 40 | | | 60 | | |

## RESULTS

___ WHITE WON          ___ DRAW          ___ BLACK WON

Notes

8
7
6
5
4
3
2
1
A B C D E F G H

| SIGNATURE | SIGNATURE |
|---|---|

# SCORE SHEET

| EVENT | | DATE | |
|---|---|---|---|
| ROUND | | BOARD | |
| SECTION | | OPENING | |
| **WHITE (name of player)** | | **BLACK (name of player)** | |

| | White | Black | | White | Black | | White | Black |
|---|---|---|---|---|---|---|---|---|
| 1 | | | 21 | | | 41 | | |
| 2 | | | 22 | | | 42 | | |
| 3 | | | 23 | | | 43 | | |
| 4 | | | 24 | | | 44 | | |
| 5 | | | 25 | | | 45 | | |
| 6 | | | 26 | | | 46 | | |
| 7 | | | 27 | | | 47 | | |
| 8 | | | 28 | | | 48 | | |
| 9 | | | 29 | | | 49 | | |
| 10 | | | 30 | | | 50 | | |
| 11 | | | 31 | | | 51 | | |
| 12 | | | 32 | | | 52 | | |
| 13 | | | 33 | | | 53 | | |
| 14 | | | 34 | | | 54 | | |
| 15 | | | 35 | | | 55 | | |
| 16 | | | 36 | | | 56 | | |
| 17 | | | 37 | | | 57 | | |
| 18 | | | 38 | | | 58 | | |
| 19 | | | 39 | | | 59 | | |
| 20 | | | 40 | | | 60 | | |

## RESULTS

___ WHITE WON    ___ DRAW    ___ BLACK WON

Notes

SIGNATURE    SIGNATURE

# SCORE SHEET

| EVENT | DATE |
|---|---|
| ROUND | BOARD |
| SECTION | OPENING |
| **WHITE (name of player)** | **BLACK (name of player)** |

| | White | Black | | White | Black | | White | Black |
|---|---|---|---|---|---|---|---|---|
| 1 | | | 21 | | | 41 | | |
| 2 | | | 22 | | | 42 | | |
| 3 | | | 23 | | | 43 | | |
| 4 | | | 24 | | | 44 | | |
| 5 | | | 25 | | | 45 | | |
| 6 | | | 26 | | | 46 | | |
| 7 | | | 27 | | | 47 | | |
| 8 | | | 28 | | | 48 | | |
| 9 | | | 29 | | | 49 | | |
| 10 | | | 30 | | | 50 | | |
| 11 | | | 31 | | | 51 | | |
| 12 | | | 32 | | | 52 | | |
| 13 | | | 33 | | | 53 | | |
| 14 | | | 34 | | | 54 | | |
| 15 | | | 35 | | | 55 | | |
| 16 | | | 36 | | | 56 | | |
| 17 | | | 37 | | | 57 | | |
| 18 | | | 38 | | | 58 | | |
| 19 | | | 39 | | | 59 | | |
| 20 | | | 40 | | | 60 | | |

## RESULTS

___ WHITE WON          ___ DRAW          ___ BLACK WON

Notes

8
7
6
5
4
3
2
1
A B C D E F G H

| SIGNATURE | SIGNATURE |
|---|---|

# SCORE SHEET

| EVENT | DATE |
|---|---|
| ROUND | BOARD |
| SECTION | OPENING |
| **WHITE (name of player)** | **BLACK (name of player)** |

| | White | Black | | White | Black | | White | Black |
|---|---|---|---|---|---|---|---|---|
| 1 | | | 21 | | | 41 | | |
| 2 | | | 22 | | | 42 | | |
| 3 | | | 23 | | | 43 | | |
| 4 | | | 24 | | | 44 | | |
| 5 | | | 25 | | | 45 | | |
| 6 | | | 26 | | | 46 | | |
| 7 | | | 27 | | | 47 | | |
| 8 | | | 28 | | | 48 | | |
| 9 | | | 29 | | | 49 | | |
| 10 | | | 30 | | | 50 | | |
| 11 | | | 31 | | | 51 | | |
| 12 | | | 32 | | | 52 | | |
| 13 | | | 33 | | | 53 | | |
| 14 | | | 34 | | | 54 | | |
| 15 | | | 35 | | | 55 | | |
| 16 | | | 36 | | | 56 | | |
| 17 | | | 37 | | | 57 | | |
| 18 | | | 38 | | | 58 | | |
| 19 | | | 39 | | | 59 | | |
| 20 | | | 40 | | | 60 | | |

## RESULTS

___ WHITE WON          ___ DRAW          ___ BLACK WON

Notes

SIGNATURE          SIGNATURE

# SCORE SHEET

| EVENT | DATE |
|---|---|
| ROUND | BOARD |
| SECTION | OPENING |
| **WHITE (name of player)** | **BLACK (name of player)** |

| | White | Black | | White | Black | | White | Black |
|---|---|---|---|---|---|---|---|---|
| 1 | | | 21 | | | 41 | | |
| 2 | | | 22 | | | 42 | | |
| 3 | | | 23 | | | 43 | | |
| 4 | | | 24 | | | 44 | | |
| 5 | | | 25 | | | 45 | | |
| 6 | | | 26 | | | 46 | | |
| 7 | | | 27 | | | 47 | | |
| 8 | | | 28 | | | 48 | | |
| 9 | | | 29 | | | 49 | | |
| 10 | | | 30 | | | 50 | | |
| 11 | | | 31 | | | 51 | | |
| 12 | | | 32 | | | 52 | | |
| 13 | | | 33 | | | 53 | | |
| 14 | | | 34 | | | 54 | | |
| 15 | | | 35 | | | 55 | | |
| 16 | | | 36 | | | 56 | | |
| 17 | | | 37 | | | 57 | | |
| 18 | | | 38 | | | 58 | | |
| 19 | | | 39 | | | 59 | | |
| 20 | | | 40 | | | 60 | | |

## RESULTS

___ WHITE WON          ___ DRAW          ___ BLACK WON

| Notes |
|---|
| |
| |
| |
| |
| |
| |
| |

| SIGNATURE | SIGNATURE |
|---|---|

# SCORE SHEET

| EVENT | | DATE | |
| ROUND | | BOARD | |
| SECTION | | OPENING | |
| **WHITE (name of player)** | | **BLACK (name of player)** | |

| | White | Black | | White | Black | | White | Black |
|---|---|---|---|---|---|---|---|---|
| 1 | | | 21 | | | 41 | | |
| 2 | | | 22 | | | 42 | | |
| 3 | | | 23 | | | 43 | | |
| 4 | | | 24 | | | 44 | | |
| 5 | | | 25 | | | 45 | | |
| 6 | | | 26 | | | 46 | | |
| 7 | | | 27 | | | 47 | | |
| 8 | | | 28 | | | 48 | | |
| 9 | | | 29 | | | 49 | | |
| 10 | | | 30 | | | 50 | | |
| 11 | | | 31 | | | 51 | | |
| 12 | | | 32 | | | 52 | | |
| 13 | | | 33 | | | 53 | | |
| 14 | | | 34 | | | 54 | | |
| 15 | | | 35 | | | 55 | | |
| 16 | | | 36 | | | 56 | | |
| 17 | | | 37 | | | 57 | | |
| 18 | | | 38 | | | 58 | | |
| 19 | | | 39 | | | 59 | | |
| 20 | | | 40 | | | 60 | | |

## RESULTS

___ WHITE WON          ___ DRAW          ___ BLACK WON

Notes

SIGNATURE          SIGNATURE

# SCORE SHEET

| EVENT | | DATE | |
|---|---|---|---|
| ROUND | | BOARD | |
| SECTION | | OPENING | |
| **WHITE (name of player)** | | **BLACK (name of player)** | |

| | White | Black | | White | Black | | White | Black |
|---|---|---|---|---|---|---|---|---|
| 1 | | | 21 | | | 41 | | |
| 2 | | | 22 | | | 42 | | |
| 3 | | | 23 | | | 43 | | |
| 4 | | | 24 | | | 44 | | |
| 5 | | | 25 | | | 45 | | |
| 6 | | | 26 | | | 46 | | |
| 7 | | | 27 | | | 47 | | |
| 8 | | | 28 | | | 48 | | |
| 9 | | | 29 | | | 49 | | |
| 10 | | | 30 | | | 50 | | |
| 11 | | | 31 | | | 51 | | |
| 12 | | | 32 | | | 52 | | |
| 13 | | | 33 | | | 53 | | |
| 14 | | | 34 | | | 54 | | |
| 15 | | | 35 | | | 55 | | |
| 16 | | | 36 | | | 56 | | |
| 17 | | | 37 | | | 57 | | |
| 18 | | | 38 | | | 58 | | |
| 19 | | | 39 | | | 59 | | |
| 20 | | | 40 | | | 60 | | |

## RESULTS

___ WHITE WON          ___ DRAW          ___ BLACK WON

Notes

SIGNATURE                    SIGNATURE

# SCORE SHEET

| EVENT | DATE |
|---|---|
| ROUND | BOARD |
| SECTION | OPENING |
| **WHITE (name of player)** | **BLACK (name of player)** |

| | White | Black | | White | Black | | White | Black |
|---|---|---|---|---|---|---|---|---|
| 1 | | | 21 | | | 41 | | |
| 2 | | | 22 | | | 42 | | |
| 3 | | | 23 | | | 43 | | |
| 4 | | | 24 | | | 44 | | |
| 5 | | | 25 | | | 45 | | |
| 6 | | | 26 | | | 46 | | |
| 7 | | | 27 | | | 47 | | |
| 8 | | | 28 | | | 48 | | |
| 9 | | | 29 | | | 49 | | |
| 10 | | | 30 | | | 50 | | |
| 11 | | | 31 | | | 51 | | |
| 12 | | | 32 | | | 52 | | |
| 13 | | | 33 | | | 53 | | |
| 14 | | | 34 | | | 54 | | |
| 15 | | | 35 | | | 55 | | |
| 16 | | | 36 | | | 56 | | |
| 17 | | | 37 | | | 57 | | |
| 18 | | | 38 | | | 58 | | |
| 19 | | | 39 | | | 59 | | |
| 20 | | | 40 | | | 60 | | |

## RESULTS

___ WHITE WON          ___ DRAW          ___ BLACK WON

Notes

SIGNATURE                    SIGNATURE

# SCORE SHEET

| EVENT | | DATE | |
|---|---|---|---|
| ROUND | | BOARD | |
| SECTION | | OPENING | |
| **WHITE (name of player)** | | **BLACK (name of player)** | |

| | White | Black | | White | Black | | White | Black |
|---|---|---|---|---|---|---|---|---|
| 1 | | | 21 | | | 41 | | |
| 2 | | | 22 | | | 42 | | |
| 3 | | | 23 | | | 43 | | |
| 4 | | | 24 | | | 44 | | |
| 5 | | | 25 | | | 45 | | |
| 6 | | | 26 | | | 46 | | |
| 7 | | | 27 | | | 47 | | |
| 8 | | | 28 | | | 48 | | |
| 9 | | | 29 | | | 49 | | |
| 10 | | | 30 | | | 50 | | |
| 11 | | | 31 | | | 51 | | |
| 12 | | | 32 | | | 52 | | |
| 13 | | | 33 | | | 53 | | |
| 14 | | | 34 | | | 54 | | |
| 15 | | | 35 | | | 55 | | |
| 16 | | | 36 | | | 56 | | |
| 17 | | | 37 | | | 57 | | |
| 18 | | | 38 | | | 58 | | |
| 19 | | | 39 | | | 59 | | |
| 20 | | | 40 | | | 60 | | |

## RESULTS

___ WHITE WON          ___ DRAW          ___ BLACK WON

Notes

SIGNATURE
SIGNATURE

# SCORE SHEET

| EVENT | | DATE | |
|---|---|---|---|
| ROUND | | BOARD | |
| SECTION | | OPENING | |
| **WHITE (name of player)** | | **BLACK (name of player)** | |

| | White | Black | | White | Black | | White | Black |
|---|---|---|---|---|---|---|---|---|
| 1 | | | 21 | | | 41 | | |
| 2 | | | 22 | | | 42 | | |
| 3 | | | 23 | | | 43 | | |
| 4 | | | 24 | | | 44 | | |
| 5 | | | 25 | | | 45 | | |
| 6 | | | 26 | | | 46 | | |
| 7 | | | 27 | | | 47 | | |
| 8 | | | 28 | | | 48 | | |
| 9 | | | 29 | | | 49 | | |
| 10 | | | 30 | | | 50 | | |
| 11 | | | 31 | | | 51 | | |
| 12 | | | 32 | | | 52 | | |
| 13 | | | 33 | | | 53 | | |
| 14 | | | 34 | | | 54 | | |
| 15 | | | 35 | | | 55 | | |
| 16 | | | 36 | | | 56 | | |
| 17 | | | 37 | | | 57 | | |
| 18 | | | 38 | | | 58 | | |
| 19 | | | 39 | | | 59 | | |
| 20 | | | 40 | | | 60 | | |

## RESULTS

___ WHITE WON        ___ DRAW        ___ BLACK WON

Notes

SIGNATURE                    SIGNATURE

# SCORE SHEET

| EVENT | | DATE | |
|---|---|---|---|
| ROUND | | BOARD | |
| SECTION | | OPENING | |
| **WHITE (name of player)** | | **BLACK (name of player)** | |

| | White | Black | | White | Black | | White | Black |
|---|---|---|---|---|---|---|---|---|
| 1 | | | 21 | | | 41 | | |
| 2 | | | 22 | | | 42 | | |
| 3 | | | 23 | | | 43 | | |
| 4 | | | 24 | | | 44 | | |
| 5 | | | 25 | | | 45 | | |
| 6 | | | 26 | | | 46 | | |
| 7 | | | 27 | | | 47 | | |
| 8 | | | 28 | | | 48 | | |
| 9 | | | 29 | | | 49 | | |
| 10 | | | 30 | | | 50 | | |
| 11 | | | 31 | | | 51 | | |
| 12 | | | 32 | | | 52 | | |
| 13 | | | 33 | | | 53 | | |
| 14 | | | 34 | | | 54 | | |
| 15 | | | 35 | | | 55 | | |
| 16 | | | 36 | | | 56 | | |
| 17 | | | 37 | | | 57 | | |
| 18 | | | 38 | | | 58 | | |
| 19 | | | 39 | | | 59 | | |
| 20 | | | 40 | | | 60 | | |

## RESULTS

___ WHITE WON          ___ DRAW          ___ BLACK WON

Notes

SIGNATURE                              SIGNATURE

# SCORE SHEET

| EVENT | DATE |
|---|---|
| ROUND | BOARD |
| SECTION | OPENING |
| **WHITE (name of player)** | **BLACK (name of player)** |

| | White | Black | | White | Black | | White | Black |
|---|---|---|---|---|---|---|---|---|
| 1 | | | 21 | | | 41 | | |
| 2 | | | 22 | | | 42 | | |
| 3 | | | 23 | | | 43 | | |
| 4 | | | 24 | | | 44 | | |
| 5 | | | 25 | | | 45 | | |
| 6 | | | 26 | | | 46 | | |
| 7 | | | 27 | | | 47 | | |
| 8 | | | 28 | | | 48 | | |
| 9 | | | 29 | | | 49 | | |
| 10 | | | 30 | | | 50 | | |
| 11 | | | 31 | | | 51 | | |
| 12 | | | 32 | | | 52 | | |
| 13 | | | 33 | | | 53 | | |
| 14 | | | 34 | | | 54 | | |
| 15 | | | 35 | | | 55 | | |
| 16 | | | 36 | | | 56 | | |
| 17 | | | 37 | | | 57 | | |
| 18 | | | 38 | | | 58 | | |
| 19 | | | 39 | | | 59 | | |
| 20 | | | 40 | | | 60 | | |

## RESULTS

___ WHITE WON          ___ DRAW          ___ BLACK WON

Notes

| SIGNATURE | SIGNATURE |
|---|---|

# SCORE SHEET

| EVENT | | DATE | |
|---|---|---|---|
| ROUND | | BOARD | |
| SECTION | | OPENING | |

**WHITE (name of player)** | | **BLACK (name of player)** |

|  | White | Black |  | White | Black |  | White | Black |
|---|---|---|---|---|---|---|---|---|
| 1 | | | 21 | | | 41 | | |
| 2 | | | 22 | | | 42 | | |
| 3 | | | 23 | | | 43 | | |
| 4 | | | 24 | | | 44 | | |
| 5 | | | 25 | | | 45 | | |
| 6 | | | 26 | | | 46 | | |
| 7 | | | 27 | | | 47 | | |
| 8 | | | 28 | | | 48 | | |
| 9 | | | 29 | | | 49 | | |
| 10 | | | 30 | | | 50 | | |
| 11 | | | 31 | | | 51 | | |
| 12 | | | 32 | | | 52 | | |
| 13 | | | 33 | | | 53 | | |
| 14 | | | 34 | | | 54 | | |
| 15 | | | 35 | | | 55 | | |
| 16 | | | 36 | | | 56 | | |
| 17 | | | 37 | | | 57 | | |
| 18 | | | 38 | | | 58 | | |
| 19 | | | 39 | | | 59 | | |
| 20 | | | 40 | | | 60 | | |

## RESULTS

___ WHITE WON          ___ DRAW          ___ BLACK WON

Notes

SIGNATURE          SIGNATURE

# SCORE SHEET

| EVENT | | DATE | |
| ROUND | | BOARD | |
| SECTION | | OPENING | |

**WHITE (name of player)** | | **BLACK (name of player)** |

| | White | Black | | White | Black | | White | Black |
|---|---|---|---|---|---|---|---|---|
| 1 | | | 21 | | | 41 | | |
| 2 | | | 22 | | | 42 | | |
| 3 | | | 23 | | | 43 | | |
| 4 | | | 24 | | | 44 | | |
| 5 | | | 25 | | | 45 | | |
| 6 | | | 26 | | | 46 | | |
| 7 | | | 27 | | | 47 | | |
| 8 | | | 28 | | | 48 | | |
| 9 | | | 29 | | | 49 | | |
| 10 | | | 30 | | | 50 | | |
| 11 | | | 31 | | | 51 | | |
| 12 | | | 32 | | | 52 | | |
| 13 | | | 33 | | | 53 | | |
| 14 | | | 34 | | | 54 | | |
| 15 | | | 35 | | | 55 | | |
| 16 | | | 36 | | | 56 | | |
| 17 | | | 37 | | | 57 | | |
| 18 | | | 38 | | | 58 | | |
| 19 | | | 39 | | | 59 | | |
| 20 | | | 40 | | | 60 | | |

## RESULTS

___ WHITE WON          ___ DRAW          ___ BLACK WON

Notes

```
8 ▓ ▓ ▓ ▓
7 ▓ ▓ ▓ ▓
6 ▓ ▓ ▓ ▓
5 ▓ ▓ ▓ ▓
4 ▓ ▓ ▓ ▓
3 ▓ ▓ ▓ ▓
2 ▓ ▓ ▓ ▓
1 ▓ ▓ ▓ ▓
  A B C D E F G H
```

SIGNATURE | SIGNATURE

# SCORE SHEET

| EVENT | | DATE | |
|---|---|---|---|
| ROUND | | BOARD | |
| SECTION | | OPENING | |
| **WHITE (name of player)** | | **BLACK (name of player)** | |

| | White | Black | | White | Black | | White | Black |
|---|---|---|---|---|---|---|---|---|
| 1 | | | 21 | | | 41 | | |
| 2 | | | 22 | | | 42 | | |
| 3 | | | 23 | | | 43 | | |
| 4 | | | 24 | | | 44 | | |
| 5 | | | 25 | | | 45 | | |
| 6 | | | 26 | | | 46 | | |
| 7 | | | 27 | | | 47 | | |
| 8 | | | 28 | | | 48 | | |
| 9 | | | 29 | | | 49 | | |
| 10 | | | 30 | | | 50 | | |
| 11 | | | 31 | | | 51 | | |
| 12 | | | 32 | | | 52 | | |
| 13 | | | 33 | | | 53 | | |
| 14 | | | 34 | | | 54 | | |
| 15 | | | 35 | | | 55 | | |
| 16 | | | 36 | | | 56 | | |
| 17 | | | 37 | | | 57 | | |
| 18 | | | 38 | | | 58 | | |
| 19 | | | 39 | | | 59 | | |
| 20 | | | 40 | | | 60 | | |

## RESULTS

___ WHITE WON          ___ DRAW          ___ BLACK WON

Notes

SIGNATURE                    SIGNATURE

# SCORE SHEET

| EVENT | DATE |
|---|---|
| ROUND | BOARD |
| SECTION | OPENING |
| **WHITE (name of player)** | **BLACK (name of player)** |

| | White | Black | | White | Black | | White | Black |
|---|---|---|---|---|---|---|---|---|
| 1 | | | 21 | | | 41 | | |
| 2 | | | 22 | | | 42 | | |
| 3 | | | 23 | | | 43 | | |
| 4 | | | 24 | | | 44 | | |
| 5 | | | 25 | | | 45 | | |
| 6 | | | 26 | | | 46 | | |
| 7 | | | 27 | | | 47 | | |
| 8 | | | 28 | | | 48 | | |
| 9 | | | 29 | | | 49 | | |
| 10 | | | 30 | | | 50 | | |
| 11 | | | 31 | | | 51 | | |
| 12 | | | 32 | | | 52 | | |
| 13 | | | 33 | | | 53 | | |
| 14 | | | 34 | | | 54 | | |
| 15 | | | 35 | | | 55 | | |
| 16 | | | 36 | | | 56 | | |
| 17 | | | 37 | | | 57 | | |
| 18 | | | 38 | | | 58 | | |
| 19 | | | 39 | | | 59 | | |
| 20 | | | 40 | | | 60 | | |

## RESULTS

___ WHITE WON          ___ DRAW          ___ BLACK WON

Notes

SIGNATURE                    SIGNATURE

# SCORE SHEET

| EVENT | | | | DATE | | | |
|---|---|---|---|---|---|---|---|
| ROUND | | | | BOARD | | | |
| SECTION | | | | OPENING | | | |
| **WHITE (name of player)** | | | | **BLACK (name of player)** | | | |

| | White | Black | | White | Black | | White | Black |
|---|---|---|---|---|---|---|---|---|
| 1 | | | 21 | | | 41 | | |
| 2 | | | 22 | | | 42 | | |
| 3 | | | 23 | | | 43 | | |
| 4 | | | 24 | | | 44 | | |
| 5 | | | 25 | | | 45 | | |
| 6 | | | 26 | | | 46 | | |
| 7 | | | 27 | | | 47 | | |
| 8 | | | 28 | | | 48 | | |
| 9 | | | 29 | | | 49 | | |
| 10 | | | 30 | | | 50 | | |
| 11 | | | 31 | | | 51 | | |
| 12 | | | 32 | | | 52 | | |
| 13 | | | 33 | | | 53 | | |
| 14 | | | 34 | | | 54 | | |
| 15 | | | 35 | | | 55 | | |
| 16 | | | 36 | | | 56 | | |
| 17 | | | 37 | | | 57 | | |
| 18 | | | 38 | | | 58 | | |
| 19 | | | 39 | | | 59 | | |
| 20 | | | 40 | | | 60 | | |

## RESULTS

___ WHITE WON        ___ DRAW        ___ BLACK WON

Notes

```
8
7
6
5
4
3
2
1
  A B C D E F G H
```

| SIGNATURE | SIGNATURE |
|---|---|

# SCORE SHEET

| EVENT | | | | DATE | | | |
|---|---|---|---|---|---|---|---|
| ROUND | | | | BOARD | | | |
| SECTION | | | | OPENING | | | |
| **WHITE (name of player)** | | | | **BLACK (name of player)** | | | |

| | White | Black | | White | Black | | White | Black |
|---|---|---|---|---|---|---|---|---|
| 1 | | | 21 | | | 41 | | |
| 2 | | | 22 | | | 42 | | |
| 3 | | | 23 | | | 43 | | |
| 4 | | | 24 | | | 44 | | |
| 5 | | | 25 | | | 45 | | |
| 6 | | | 26 | | | 46 | | |
| 7 | | | 27 | | | 47 | | |
| 8 | | | 28 | | | 48 | | |
| 9 | | | 29 | | | 49 | | |
| 10 | | | 30 | | | 50 | | |
| 11 | | | 31 | | | 51 | | |
| 12 | | | 32 | | | 52 | | |
| 13 | | | 33 | | | 53 | | |
| 14 | | | 34 | | | 54 | | |
| 15 | | | 35 | | | 55 | | |
| 16 | | | 36 | | | 56 | | |
| 17 | | | 37 | | | 57 | | |
| 18 | | | 38 | | | 58 | | |
| 19 | | | 39 | | | 59 | | |
| 20 | | | 40 | | | 60 | | |

## RESULTS

___ WHITE WON  ___ DRAW  ___ BLACK WON

Notes

SIGNATURE

SIGNATURE

# SCORE SHEET

| EVENT | DATE |
|---|---|
| ROUND | BOARD |
| SECTION | OPENING |
| **WHITE (name of player)** | **BLACK (name of player)** |

| | White | Black | | White | Black | | White | Black |
|---|---|---|---|---|---|---|---|---|
| 1 | | | 21 | | | 41 | | |
| 2 | | | 22 | | | 42 | | |
| 3 | | | 23 | | | 43 | | |
| 4 | | | 24 | | | 44 | | |
| 5 | | | 25 | | | 45 | | |
| 6 | | | 26 | | | 46 | | |
| 7 | | | 27 | | | 47 | | |
| 8 | | | 28 | | | 48 | | |
| 9 | | | 29 | | | 49 | | |
| 10 | | | 30 | | | 50 | | |
| 11 | | | 31 | | | 51 | | |
| 12 | | | 32 | | | 52 | | |
| 13 | | | 33 | | | 53 | | |
| 14 | | | 34 | | | 54 | | |
| 15 | | | 35 | | | 55 | | |
| 16 | | | 36 | | | 56 | | |
| 17 | | | 37 | | | 57 | | |
| 18 | | | 38 | | | 58 | | |
| 19 | | | 39 | | | 59 | | |
| 20 | | | 40 | | | 60 | | |

## RESULTS

___ WHITE WON            ___ DRAW            ___ BLACK WON

Notes

8
7
6
5
4
3
2
1
A B C D E F G H

| SIGNATURE | SIGNATURE |
|---|---|

# NOTES

_____

_____

_____

_____

_____

_____

_____

_____

_____

_____

_____

_____

_____

_____

_____

_____

_____

_____

_____

_____

_____

_____

NOTES

_____

_____

_____

_____

_____

_____

_____

_____

_____

_____

_____

_____

_____

_____

_____

_____

_____

_____

_____

_____

_____

# NOTES

# NOTES

_____

_____

_____

_____

_____

_____

_____

_____

_____

_____

_____

_____

_____

_____

_____

_____

_____

_____

_____

_____

_____

_____

# NOTES

NOTES

NOTES

# NOTES

Made in the USA
Las Vegas, NV
13 July 2024

92272808R10063